In the Know

UNDERSTANDING AND USING IDIOMS

Cindy Leaney

CAMBRIDGE UNIVERSITY PRESS
Cambridge, New York, Melbourne, Madrid, Cape Town, Singapore, São Paulo

Cambridge University Press
40 West 20th Street, New York, NY 10011-4211, USA

www.cambridge.org

Information on this title: www.cambridge.org/9780521545426

First published 2005

Printed in the United States of America
A catalog record for this publication is available from the British Library.

Library of Congress Cataloging-in-Publication Data

Leaney, Cindy.
In the know : understanding and using idioms / Cindy Leaney.
p. cm.
ISBN-13: 978-0-521-54542-6
ISBN-10: 0-521-54542-0
1. English language—Idioms—Problems, exercises, etc. 2. English language—Textbooks for foreign speakers. I. Title.

PE1128.L367 2005
428.2'4--dc22

2005045721

ISBN-13 978-0-521-54542-6 paperback
ISBN-10 0-521-54542-0 paperback

Art direction, book design, and layout services: Adventure House, NYC
Illustrations: Stephen Quinlan

Contents

Acknowledgments

I would like to thank:
Paul Heacock for getting the ball rolling, and being there for the long haul.
Bernard D. Seal for his valuable help in getting the project off the ground.
Nóirín Burke and Joe McVeigh for putting their two cents in.
Heather McCarron for staying on top of production issues.
And Tony Leaney for his help and encouragement day in, day out.

I would also like to thank the reviewers of *In the Know* for helping us keep our fingers on the pulse of what teachers want and need for the ESL classroom:
Janette L. MacDonald, International Education Services, Tokyo, Japan
Sarah Wilkins Zovich, English Language Institute, Holy Cross College, Notre Dame, Indiana
Lorenzo Fantini, Simul Academy Shinjuku, Tokyo, Japan
Suzanne House, English Language Institute, Lakeland College, Sheboygan, Wisconsin

Introduction

Idiomatic English is fun, interesting, and colorful. Your English will sound more natural when you can use idioms successfully. You will be able to understand more of what you read and hear too.

This book is designed to help you feel more confident using idioms and to give you more control over them by understanding their meaning, their grammar, how they look and sound, and when and where to use them.

What is an idiom?

An idiom is a group of words. As a group, the words combine to form a new meaning. The words work as a team.

For example, you know the meaning of *house* and *cards*, and you probably know what the literal (basic) meaning of a *house of cards* is:

The idiomatic meaning – an organization or plan that is very weak and can easily be destroyed – is not obvious.

Are idioms formal or informal?

Idioms are common in both formal and informal spoken and written English. There is a section in each unit called ***Focus on use*** to help you know when and how to use the idioms appropriately.

There are also "Play it safe" icons – ⚠ – to tell you to be careful when using certain idioms.

Recognizing idioms

A combination of your knowledge of the world, context clues, and common sense can help you recognize and understand idioms when you read or hear them.

What are context clues?

Context clues are other words or phrases in a text that help you recognize that a group of words may be an idiom and help you guess its meaning. Context clues usually appear very near the idiom – either in the same sentence or in the sentence immediately following the idiom. There are several different types of context clues.

- There may be *example* clues, i.e., words or phrases that give details of what the idiom is describing:

The school is coming apart at the seams. *Several good teachers have left, more and more students are dropping out,* and *the building is about to fall down.*

The school is in a bad condition. The signs of this are that "several good teachers have left, more and more students are dropping out, and the building is about to fall down."

- There may be other words or phrases before or after the idiom that *mean the same thing* as the idiom:

After my first question, Mack just clammed up and *didn't say another word*.

After my first question, Mack stopped talking completely – he "didn't say another word."

- A sentence may contain a *comparison* or *contrast* clue:

Mike and Jane don't see eye to eye, but Jane and I *agree on everything*.

Mike and Jane don't agree, <u>but</u> Jane and I "agree on everything."

- There may be *experience* or *situation* clues:

Trying to find a *small plane* in this *rain forest* is like looking for a needle in a haystack.

Trying to find a small plane in this rain forest is very difficult because it is looking for something small in a very big space.

How does this book work?

In the Know units are grouped into three parts: ***Contexts***, ***Concepts***, and ***Key words***.

The ***Context*** units contain idioms that are used in topics or situations like travel, work, or eating and drinking.

The idioms in the ***Concept*** units are linked by a common theme, such as danger, ability, or success.

Idioms in the ***Key word*** units are grouped by similar words in the idioms themselves, rather than their meaning, for example, colors or parts of the body.

Each unit has a presentation section of idioms and their meanings. Listen to the presentation section on the **audio CD** when you start a new unit.

The presentation section is followed by an activities section, which practices the **meaning**, **form** (grammar, spelling, pronunciation), and **use** (register and appropriacy, personalization) of the idioms.

The ***Reference* section** is based on the ***Cambridge Dictionary of American Idioms*** and includes full definitions of all the idioms in the book with example sentences and usage notes.

Unit 1

Agreeing and disagreeing

Jeff: This is the worst coffee in town.

Maria: You can say that again.

Cathy: And how!

Maria: We should sound out the boss about getting a new machine.

Jeff: You have got to be kidding. There's no way she'd agree.

Cathy: Somebody has to speak up.

Jeff: Let's talk about it at the next staff meeting.

Maria: OK. You say your piece, and then I'll put my two cents in.

Cathy: Excellent! We are definitely on the same wavelength!

Agreeing

- **and how,** *also* **you bet** *or* **you can say that again** I agree
- **on the same wavelength,** *also* **see eye to eye** to agree or have the same opinion of something

Disagreeing

- **you must be kidding,** *also* **you have got to be kidding** you are not being serious, *or* I do not agree with you
- **take issue with someone / something** [slightly formal] to disagree
- **at odds** to be in disagreement
- **on the contrary** just the opposite of what has been said or believed

Opinions

- **put your two cents in,** *also* **say your piece** *or* **speak up** to give your opinion
- **sound out someone** to find out what someone's opinion about something is
- **win someone over** to succeed in changing someone's opinion
- **where someone is coming from** what causes someone to have a particular opinion

Focus on meaning

A *Grouping*

Put the idioms in the box into the correct group.

a. and how	f. say your piece	k. you bet
b. at odds	g. see eye to eye	l. you can say that again
c. on the contrary	h. sound out someone	m. you must / have got to be kidding
d. on the same wavelength	i. speak up	
e. put your two cents in	j. take issue with	

Agreeing

a. and how

....

....

....

....

Disagreeing

....

....

....

....

Giving opinions

....

....

....

....

B *Matching*

Match the idioms with their definitions.

1. on the contrary
2. see eye to eye
3. where someone is coming from
4. speak up
5. sound out someone
6. you bet
7. win somebody over, *also* win over somebody

a. I agree
b. just the opposite, especially of something said or believed
c. to agree with someone
d. to carefully discover what someone thinks or knows
e. to express your opinion
f. to succeed in changing someone's opinion
g. what causes someone to have a particular opinion

Focus on form

A *Scrambled sentences*

Put the words in these sentences into the correct order.

1. That is one eye issue on we eye to see.

   That is one issue we see eye to eye on.

2. You kidding have to be got!

3. On the, think we it's a idea very contrary good.

4. two Can just I my cents put in?

5. that say again You can.

6. you If agree, up speak don't.

B *Sentence completion*

Write in the missing word in each sentence.

1. We work well together because we are on the ___same___ wavelength.
2. Well, I'm afraid I have to take ______ with you there.
3. She won them ______ by explaining her point of view.
4. I can understand ______ you're coming from.
5. I ______ issue with some of their decisions.
6. Let's sound ______ the board at the next meeting.
7. They have been at odds ______ one another since Dave joined the company.
8. I said my ______ and then waited for their reaction.
9. "I think we should buy two." "______ bet!"
10. "That was a great movie." "______ how!"

Focus on use

A *Formality*

Which is the better thing to say in each of these situations? Consider how formal or informal each conversation is.

1. You are with friends, trying to decide where to go for dinner. They disagree with each other. You have an idea that you think both of them will like.
   a. Can I put my two cents in?
   b. May I express an opinion?
2. You are in a formal meeting with several people from different companies. Your boss says something you strongly disagree with.
   a. You have got to be kidding!
   b. I'd have to take issue with you there.
3. You are walking out of class after a difficult test. One of your classmates says, "That was a tough test!"
   a. You can say that again!
   b. I strongly agree.

B *Over to you*

With a partner, choose a topic from the list below. Decide whether you agree or disagree. Make notes about different points you can make. Then use some of the idioms from this unit as you discuss the topic with your partner.

Cigarette smoking should be made a crime.

Parents should not control their children's access to the Internet.

Extreme sports are dangerous and should be banned.

Now write

Write a dialog among three friends on the topic discussed in ***Over to you***. Use as many idioms from the unit as you can.

Unit 2

Communicating

Bob: Hi. I thought I'd call and touch base. How are the party plans going?

Gloria: Well, just between you and me, there's a problem. It's Matt. I think he got wind of the surprise party.

Bob: How?

Gloria: I don't know. Somebody who's in the loop may have let him in on it. I'll see him later and try to find out. I won't beat around the bush. I'll say, "What are you doing for your birthday?" I'll be in touch as soon as I've seen him.

Talking and telling

- **open up** to talk about things freely and honestly
- **between you and me** private
- **let someone in on something** to tell someone a secret
- **compare notes** to share opinions with someone
- **touch base (with someone)** to talk to someone briefly
- **pick up on something** to continue to talk about something that someone said earlier in the conversation
- **beat around the bush** to avoid talking about something by talking about other things
- **bend someone's ear** to talk to someone for a long time
- **get through (to somebody)** to reach someone by phone

Listening to or trying to get someone to talk

- **draw someone out** to try to make someone talk about his or her feelings
- **lend an ear (to someone)** to listen to someone

Not talking

- **bite your tongue**, *also* **hold your tongue** to stop yourself from speaking, usually because it might cause problems if you spoke
- **clam up** to refuse to talk

Receiving information

- **get wind of something** to find out about something that was secret or not known before
- **in touch (with someone)** communicating with that person
- **in the loop** included in the sharing of information

Focus on meaning

A *Grouping*

Put the idioms in the box into the correct group.

a. clam up	c. get wind of something	e. let someone in on something
b. compare notes	d. lend an ear to someone	f. open up

Listening to or trying to get someone to talk

draw someone out

....

Not talking

hold your tongue

....

Talking and telling

beat around the bush
bend someone's ear
pick up on
touch base with someone

b. compare notes

....

....

Receiving information

in the loop
in touch (with someone)

....

B *Matching*

Match the idioms with their definitions.

a. beat around the bush	d. get through (to somebody)	g. pick up on something
b. between you and me	e. in the loop	h. touch base (with someone)
c. draw someone out	f. in touch (with someone)	

1. having knowledge of and involvement in something e
2. in communication with someone .....
3. to avoid talking about what is important .....
4. to make contact with someone by telephone .....
5. to persuade someone to express his or her thoughts and feelings .....
6. to talk briefly to someone .....
7. private .....
8. to continue talking about something .....

Focus on form

A *Communication crossword*

Complete the crossword by filling in the missing word in each idiom.

Across

3 ______ notes (7)

4 ______ you and me (7)

6 ______ someone in on something (3)

7 ______ up on something (4)

Down

1 ______ someone out (4)

2 ______ up (4)

4 ______ your tongue (4)

5 ______ base (5)

6 in the ______ (4)

8 ______ touch (2)

B *Correct or incorrect?*

Are these sentences correct? Put a check (✔) in the box if the sentence is correct. Put an ✘ in the box and correct the idiom if it is wrong.

1. Stay on touch! ☒ Stay in touch!
2. Stop beating along the bush. ☐ ______
3. He's always bending someone's ear about his car. ☐ ______
4. She started to tell us, but then she just clammed up. ☐ ______
5. He really opened and talked about everything. ☐ ______
6. How did he get wind of the surprise party? ☐ ______
7. You can probably get through to her on her cell phone. ☐ ______
8. She's always ready to loan an ear when it's needed. ☐ ______

Focus on use

A *Formality*

Rewrite this detective story to make it sound more natural by replacing the words in blue with idioms from the box. You may need to change the tense of some verbs.

beat around the bush | clam up | compare notes | get wind of

It was late, and I was tired. I had been trying to get Mack to talk, but after my first question, he just refused to talk anymore (1) ______________.

"Look, Mack, I'm not going to avoid talking about it (2) ______________ anymore. I think I know what happened that night.

"You met your old pal Tommy to exchange information and opinions (3) ______________. Both of you had learned about (4) ______________ the robbery. You woke up the next morning, but Tommy didn't. Tell me why. Now!"

B *Over to you*

1. *When we talk about communicating in English, we often use the ideas of "open" and "closed" to describe whether someone is willing to communicate or not. Is it the same in your language?*
2. *In some languages and cultures, it is OK to talk at the same time as someone else. In others, people take turns in a conversation. What is polite in your language?*

Now write

Do you like to communicate in person – **face to face** – or by phone or e-mail? Write a paragraph about how you like to stay in touch with friends. Use some of the idioms in the unit.

Eating and drinking

Mandy: You said you were going to whip something up, not prepare a feast!

Pamela: Well, we don't get to break bread with each other that often. And it's a special day.

José: Yes, it is. Let's drink to Dave and Mandy!

Pamela: Absolutely! Let's break out the champagne!

(a bit later)

Dave: That was fantastic – salmon washed down with champagne.

Mandy: I'm afraid I really stuffed myself with the salmon. It was delicious.

José: I really pigged out, too. Wonderful.

Eating

- **break bread with someone** to eat together
- ⚠ **eat like a horse** to eat a lot of food often
- **eat someone out of house and home** to eat a lot of food in someone's home
- ⚠ **pig out** to eat a lot
- **put away food or drinks** to eat or drink a lot of something
- ⚠ **stuff your face** to eat a lot quickly or continuously
- **pick at food** to eat in small pieces without enjoyment

Drinking

- **drink to someone / something** to take a drink (usually of alcohol) to wish good health or good luck to someone or something
- **drown your sorrows** to drink a lot of alcohol to stop feeling sad
- **tank up on something** to drink a lot of something
- **wash something down** to drink liquid to help swallow food or medicine

Preparing and serving food and drink

- **break out something,** *also* **break something out** to serve food or drinks to people
- **whip up something,** *also* **whip something up** to quickly prepare something to eat

Focus on meaning

A *Matching*

Match the idioms with their definitions.

1. break bread with someone
2. drown your sorrows
3. whip up something *or* whip something up
4. stuff your face
5. break out something
6. tank up on something
7. wash down something
8. drink to someone
9. eat like a horse
10. put away food or drinks

a. to serve food or drink
b. to eat with someone
c. to drink a lot of alcohol to stop feeling sad
d. to eat or drink a lot of something
e. to drink a liquid to help you swallow something
f. to eat a lot of food quickly or continuously
g. to eat a lot of food often
h. to quickly prepare something to eat
i. to drink a great deal of something
j. to wish good health or good luck to someone

B *Sentence completion*

Use idioms from the box to complete the following sentences. You may have to change the form of some words.

eat like a horse	pick at something	whip up something
eat someone out of house and home	pig out	

1. We got back from the airport, and Claudia ___whipped up___ a snack for all of us.
2. The teenagers were home for only three days, but they nearly ________.
3. Alex was very hungry and really ________ at lunch.
4. She didn't seem too hungry – she just sat there and ________ her food.
5. The food was great, and we all ________.

Focus on form

A *Prepositions and adverbs*

Use the prepositions and adverbs in the box to complete the sentences. You may need to use some prepositions more than once.

at	away	down	into	on	out	to	up	with

1. I wish we could break bread ___with___ each other more often.
2. Let's drink ______ the new company.
3. I think they put ______ two pizzas each!
4. Take two aspirins washed ______ ______ plenty of water.
5. Tank ______ ______ juice and water before we go to the beach.
6. Why are you picking ______ your food? Aren't you hungry?
7. Let's break ______ the dessert!

B *Scrambled sentences*

Put the words in these sentences into the correct order.

1. she stays eats but thin like She a horse. (*two possible ways*)

   She eats like a horse but she stays thin. or She stays thin but she eats like a horse.

2. good idea Drowning not your sorrows is a.

   ______

3. go Let's and home whip up I'll something. (*two possible ways*)

   ______

4. with They us for two home ate weeks stayed and and us out of house.

   ______

5. popcorn We the faces movies and went stuffed to our with.

   ______

6. She out likes to on pig food junk sometimes. (*two possible ways*)

   ______

Focus on use

A *Formality*

Which of these idioms are appropriate (right or correct to use) in these social situations? Write the letter of the idiom(s) under each situation. You may use an idiom more than once.

a. break bread with someone
b. break out something
c. drink to someone / something
d. drown your sorrows
e. eat like a horse
f. eat someone out of house and home
g. pick at something
h. pig out
i. put away
j. stuff your face
k. tank up on
l. wash down
m. whip something up *or* whip up something

1. You have a new job. Your boss has invited you to dinner.

....

2. You are having lunch at your house with good friends you see often.

....

3. You are giving a welcome speech to foreign visitors before a formal business breakfast.

....

4. You have new neighbors. You have invited them over for lunch at your house.

....

B *Over to you*

Answer the following questions about eating and drinking in your own language.

1. *Is there a common phrase that means something like to* ***break bread with someone****? What is it?*
2. *When you are talking about someone who eats a lot, would you ever say the person* ***eats like a horse*** *or any other animal?*

Now write

Write a short dialog between two friends who are talking about a party they both enjoyed. Use idioms from the unit.

Unit 4

Feelings

Yesterday I got up on the wrong side of the bed. I'd been feeling down in the dumps since I quit my job.

At first, I enjoyed advertising. I worked hard and I loved it. Then I changed companies.

My new boss began to drive me up the wall. She was always blowing hot and cold about my project proposals. One minute she was positive. The next minute she wasn't interested. I was on edge all the time. It was time for something new. My heart just wasn't in it anymore. So I quit and applied to work overseas as a volunteer.

After breakfast I went to check the mail. There was a big envelope on the floor. That was a sight for sore eyes! I opened it.

I got a job in Africa! I'm going to teach in Africa for two years! Suddenly, I was walking on air!

Feeling unhappy

- ⚠ **get up on the wrong side of (the) bed** to start the day feeling unhappy or uncomfortable
- **down in the dumps** feeling unhappy

Feeling happy or good

- **over the moon,** *also* **walking on air** to be very happy
- **a sight for sore eyes** something that you are happy to see
- **whatever floats your boat** to do whatever makes you happy
- **pick you up** to make you feel happier
- **be swept away** *or* **carried away (by something)** to feel very enthusiastic or emotional

Feeling emotional

- **have a lump in your throat,** *also* **get choked up** to feel very emotional
- **cool down,** *also* **cool off** to stop feeling angry or emotional
- **blow hot and cold** to be positive sometimes and sometimes negative
- **your heart isn't in something** you aren't interested in or excited about it
- **on edge** nervous or worried
- **out of sorts** in a bad mood
- **up in arms** very angry
- **touch a (raw) nerve,** *also* **hit a (raw) nerve** to cause an emotional reaction
- ⚠ **drive someone up the wall** to make someone very unhappy, angry, or anxious

Focus on meaning

A *Positive or negative?*

Are these idioms used to describe positive or negative feelings? Put a check in the correct column.

Idiom	Positive	Negative
1. a sight for sore eyes	✓	
2. down in the dumps		
3. get up on the wrong side of bed		
4. out of sorts		
5. over the moon		
6. something drives you up the wall		
7. walking on air		
8. your heart isn't in something		

B *Sentence completion*

Use idioms from the box to complete the following sentences. You may have to change the form of some words.

blow hot and cold	a lump in your throat	up in arms
carried away	on edge	whatever floats your boat
choked up	pick you up	
cool off	touch a raw nerve	

1. "I'm going to take a year off and travel." "Great. whatever floats your boat!"
2. Most people are a little ______ before an important exam.
3. The boss is still angry. Give her a chance to ______.
4. He can't decide how he feels about this idea – he's been ______ for weeks.
5. It was a sad play. I had ______ at the end.
6. We got ______ and invited the whole class to the party.
7. Parents are ______ over plans to close the school.
8. The winner wanted to say a few words, but he got ______ and couldn't speak.
9. The sunshine really ______, doesn't it?
10. The decision to raise tuition ______ among the students.

Focus on form

A *Prepositions and adverbs*

Use the prepositions and adverbs in the box to complete the sentences. You will need to use some of these words more than once.

away	down	in	of	on	over	up

1. Let's take a break and give everyone a chance to cool down.
2. Turn that music off! It is driving me .... the wall.
3. He's still teaching, but his heart isn't .... his job anymore.
4. Every time I hear that song, I get a lump .... my throat.
5. We were .... the moon when we heard the news!
6. She's been feeling out .... sorts for a few days.
7. It's easy to get swept .... by the holiday spirit.
8. I got .... the wrong side .... bed this morning.
9. It's great. I'm walking .... air.
10. That song always chokes me ....

B *Correct or incorrect?*

Are these sentences correct? Put a check (✔) in the box if the sentence is correct. Put an ✘ in the box and correct the idiom if it is wrong.

1. Are you off edge before an exam? ☒ Are you on edge before an exam?
2. We are up on arms about the plan. ☐ ....
3. She knows what floats her boat. ☐ ....
4. Don't get too carried away. ☐ ....
5. He's up in the dumps. ☐ ....
6. He blows cold and hot all the time. ☐ ....
7. Winning really picked up. ☐ ....
8. You're a sight for sore ears! ☐ ....
9. Seeing her touched a raw nerve. ☐ ....

Focus on use

A *Formality*

Rewrite this dialog to make it sound more natural by replacing the words in blue with idioms from the box. You may have to change the form of some words.

down in the dumps	pick (someone) up
driving me up the wall	up in arms
on edge	a sight for sore eyes

Lynn: Hi! You're looking a little sad (1) ____________. What's the matter?

Jaime: I guess I've been a bit nervous and worried (2) ____________.

Lynn: Why?

Jaime: It's the new manager. He's really making me angry (3) ____________.

Lynn: What's he doing?

Jaime: He's very angry (4) ____________ over last month's sales figures.

Lynn: Well, then these new figures will be something that you're happy to see (5) ____________.

Jaime: Great! Fantastic! Lynn, that's really made me feel happy (6) ____________!

B *Over to you*

1. *Is there a common phrase in your language with the same meaning as **walking on air**? What is it?*
2. *What advice would you give to someone who is **on edge** most of the time?*

Now write

Write about a time when something was **a sight for sore eyes** for you.

Unit 5

Expressing emotions

Sue: What's so funny?

Linda: I just saw Jo. I knew there was something wrong. She always wears her heart on her sleeve. I asked if there was something she wanted to get off her chest. She burst into tears.

Sue: What was it?

Linda: She broke a nail. It was hard to keep a straight face.

Sue: What did you say?

Linda: I said, "Get a grip. It's a fingernail." She saw the funny side, and we were in gales of laughter.

Sue: She's been working too hard. She probably just needed to let off a little steam.

Linda: Yeah, I think you're right. She was all smiles by the time she left.

Showing happiness

- **light up** to suddenly look happy
- **be all smiles** to smile a lot
- **gales of laughter** loud, happy sounds that a group of people make when they are amused

Laughing and crying

- **burst into tears** to suddenly start to cry
- **dissolve into tears / laughter** to start to cry or laugh helplessly

Communicating your feelings

- **blow off steam,** *also* **let off steam** to do or say something to help you get rid of strong emotions
- **bare your soul** to tell someone your secret thoughts and feelings
- **get something off your chest** to tell someone about something that has been worrying you
- **wear your heart on your sleeve** to show your feelings, especially your love for someone

Controlling your emotions

- **lower your guard,** *also* **drop your guard** to stop being careful about sharing your emotions
- **lose your head** to lose control of your emotions
- **lose your temper** to become very angry
- **go ballistic** to become extremely upset
- **throw a tantrum** to become very angry and unreasonable
- **get a grip (on yourself)** to get control over your emotions
- **keep a straight face** to try not to smile or laugh

Focus on meaning

A *Matching*

Match the idioms with their definitions.

a. bare your soul
b. blow off steam, *also* let off steam
c. burst into tears
d. drop your guard, *also* lower your guard
e. get a grip (on yourself)
f. get something off your chest
g. keep a straight face
h. light up
i. throw a tantrum
j. wear your heart on your sleeve

1. to avoid showing any emotion, especially amusement g. keep a straight face
2. to become very angry and unreasonable ……………
3. to control your emotions ……………
4. to do or say something that helps you get rid of strong feelings or emotions ……………
5. to express your secret thoughts and feelings ……………
6. to look happy ……………
7. to show your feelings, especially your love for someone ……………
8. to stop being careful about expressing your emotions ……………
9. to cry suddenly ……………
10. to tell someone about something that has been worrying you ……………

B *Grouping*

Put the idioms in the box into the correct group.

be all smiles	dissolve into tears	go ballistic	light up
dissolve into laughter	get a grip (on yourself)	keep a straight face	lose your head

Expressing happiness

be all smiles
……………
……………

Controlling emotions

……………
……………

Expressing sadness / anger

……………
……………
……………

Focus on form

A *Feelings crossword*

Complete the crossword by filling in the missing word in each idiom.

Across

3 She wears her heart on her .... (6)

4 It was hard to keep a .... face. (8)

8 Oh! Get a ....! (4)

9 Don't worry. He's just letting off .... (5)

Down

1 We looked at each other and .... into laughter. (9)

2 Is there something you'd like to get off your ....? (5)

4 Everything's fine. She's all .... now. (6)

5 Remember: don't lower your .... at all. (5)

6 I'm sorry I lost my .... (6)

7 You shouldn't .... your soul to just anyone. (4)

B *Correct or incorrect?*

Are these sentences correct? Put a check (✔) in the box if the sentence is correct. Put an ✘ in the box and correct the idiom if it is wrong.

1. When his computer crashed, he went ballistic! ☑ ....
2. There were gales of tears coming from the classroom. ☐ ....
3. She looked at the report and burst into tears. ☐ ....
4. Suddenly their faces just lit down. ☐ ....
5. He threw a tantrum in the supermarket. ☐ ....
6. They discussed into tears when they heard the news. ☐ ....
7. I was so scared. I just lost my head. ☐ ....
8. Exercise is a great way to let off steam. ☐ ....

Focus on use

A *Sentence completion*

Use idioms from the unit to complete this e-mail from Jane to her friend Pete.

New Message

To: Pete

From: Jane

Subject: Thanks!

It was great to see you last week. I'm sorry I (1) .... my .... in the restaurant. I didn't mean to (2) .... like that. The poor waiter probably thought I was crazy. I've been traveling a lot since I started this new job, and I haven't had anyone to talk to.

I think I just needed to (3) .... things .... and (4) .... some ....

Thanks for being such a great friend.

B *Over to you*

Answer the following questions. As you do so, try to use some of the idioms presented in this unit.

1. *Have you ever been in a situation where you needed to* ***keep a straight face****? What happened?*
2. *In most cultures there are rules about when, where, and how people can* ***let off steam****. What are the rules in your home culture?*

Now write

Write a short, short story about someone expressing strong emotions. Use idioms from the unit. The story can be real or imagined.

Unit 6

Fighting and arguing

Sara: You know, Richard and James have had this running battle for months. Last night James really let Richard have it. I thought they were going to come to blows.

Diane: Really? That sounds serious.

Sara: Richard walks in, spoiling for a fight. He says, "It's time we had this out." James looks up and says, "Are you sure you want to take me on?" Richard says, "Yeah, I'm sure." "Bring it on," says James. Then they went at it – hot and heavy.

Diane: Wow.

Sara: Yeah, it was the most exciting game of Ping-Pong I've ever seen!

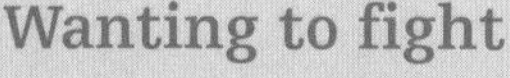

Wanting to fight

- **spoiling for a fight** very eager to fight
- **take on someone,** *also* **take someone on** to choose to fight or compete with someone

Starting a fight

- **pick a fight,** *also* **start something** to begin a fight
- **go at someone,** *also* **go at it** *or* **let someone have it** to attack someone physically or with words
- **let fly with something** to say something that will make someone angry
- ⚠ **bring it on** to begin a fight or a competition

Fighting

- **fight it out** to argue or fight until an agreement is reached
- **have it out (with someone)** to argue or fight with someone who has made you angry
- **come to blows** to begin to fight physically
- **take the gloves off** to start fighting or arguing in a more determined way
- **a running battle** an argument that continues for a long time
- **hot and heavy** full of strong emotion

Preventing a fight

- **keep the peace** [slightly formal] to stop an argument or a fight from happening

Focus on meaning

A *Which idiom?*

Read the dictionary definition and decide which idiom it describes.

1. to attack someone physically or with words
   a. hot and heavy
   b. a running battle
   c. let someone have it

2. full of strong feelings
   a. a running battle
   b. pick a fight
   c. hot and heavy

3. to attack or fight with someone
   a. spoiling for a fight
   b. hot and heavy
   c. go at someone

4. to be very eager to fight or argue
   a. spoiling for a fight
   b. take the gloves off
   c. a running battle

5. to prevent fighting or difficulties
   a. let fly with something
   b. take the gloves off
   c. keep the peace

6. to have a fight or serious argument
   a. let fly with something
   b. come to blows
   c. keep the peace

7. to begin a fight or an argument
   a. start something
   b. come to blows
   c. keep the peace

8. to express yourself in a way that will excite or anger others
   a. let fly with something
   b. come to blows
   c. keep the peace

B *Matching*

Decide what the one missing word is in all the definitions. Then match the idioms with their definitions.

1. bring it on
2. fight it out
3. have it out (with someone)
4. take on someone
5. a running battle
6. pick a fight (with someone)
7. take the gloves off

a. to argue or .... until agreement is reached
b. to argue or .... with someone who has made you angry
c. to argue, compete, or .... even more strongly
d. an argument or a .... that continues for a long time
e. to begin a .... or a competition
f. to .... or compete against someone
g. to start a .... or an argument with someone

Focus on form

A *Prepositions*

Use the prepositions in the box to complete the sentences. You will need to use some of them more than once.

at	for	off	on	out	to	with

1. We're ready when you are. Bring it ___on___!
2. Martin's always spoiling ________ a fight.
3. I think it's time we had this ________ once and for all.
4. Do you really think you're ready to take them ________?
5. There is absolutely no reason to come ________ blows.
6. It was a friendly discussion until their lawyers took the gloves ________.
7. Listen to them argue. They've been going ________ it for an hour.
8. Suddenly, he let fly ________ angry threats.

B *Scrambled sentences*

Put the words in these sentences into the correct order.

1. had battle for a years They've running.

   They've had a running battle for years.

2. argument The heavy is and hot.

   ____

3. really She it let have him!

   ____

4. peace tried The the referees to keep.

   ____

5. to you start want Do something?

   ____

6. with him pick a fight Don't!

   ____

Focus on use

A *Time line*

These idioms name parts or stages in an argument. Where does each idiom fit best?

come to blows	hot and heavy	pick a fight	take the gloves off
fight it out	let someone have it	start something	

Stage I	When people are about to begin fighting	1. spoiling for a fight 2. .... 3. ....
Stage II	The early stages of an argument or fight	4. take someone on 5. .... 6. ....
Stage III	The main part of the argument or fight	7. going at it 8. .... 9. .... 10. ....

B *Over to you*

1. *Do you think it's healthy or good to argue sometimes? When?*
2. *Is there a common phrase in your language that means the same as* ***pick a fight****?*

Now write

Write about an argument or a competition that you have seen or heard about. Use idioms from the unit.

Unit 7

Health

I wasn't feeling well. Maybe something I ate didn't agree with me. Maybe the flu was going around. I wasn't at death's door, but I was definitely not up to par. So I went to see the doctor.

"There's nothing wrong with you," the doctor said. He gave me a clean bill of health. But I knew he was wrong.

I got home and called a friend. "OK. What are your symptoms?" she asked.

"I'm really tired. I've got bags under my eyes."

"I think you're just tired, and work is stressing you out," said my friend. "You need a vacation. It will do you a world of good."

"You're right. Hey! I'm feeling better already."

Feeling good and healthy

- **a clean bill of health** to have nothing wrong
- **do you a world of good** to make you feel better

Feeling sick or unhealthy

- **not up to par**, *also* **below par** not feeling as good as you usually feel
- **under the weather** not feeling well
- **stress you out** to make you feel nervous
- **worn out** very tired
- **not agree with you**, *also* **upset your stomach** to make you feel sick
- **come down with something** to begin to get sick

Symptoms [signs that you aren't well]

- **fight something off** to try not to get sick
- ⚠ **have bags under your eyes** to have dark circles under your eyes
- **run a fever** to have a higher than normal temperature
- **going around** said of an illness that is affecting many people

Being seriously ill

- **fighting for your life** in danger of dying
- ⚠ **have one foot in the grave**, *also* **at death's door** seriously ill and likely to die soon

Recovering

- **on the mend** feeling better after an illness or injury
- **get over an illness** to get well or stop being sick
- **get back on your feet** to recover and feel healthy again

Learn more about idioms to describe "good" and "bad" in Unit 26.

Focus on meaning

A *Connections*

Use a phrase in the box as the heading for each group of related idioms.

become healthier	feel weak or ill	resist an illness
become ill	feel well	seriously ill
cause you to feel ill	make you feel good	signs that you are not well

1. feel well
   have a clean bill of health
   feel up to par

2. ....
   do you a world of good

3. ....
   feel below par
   be stressed out
   be under the weather
   be worn out

4. ....
   fight for your life
   have one foot in the grave
   at death's door

5. ....
   not agree with you
   upset your stomach

6. ....
   fight something off

7. ....
   come down with something

8. ....
   have bags under your eyes
   run a fever

9. ....
   get over it
   get back on your feet
   be on the mend

B *Scrambled dialog*

In the dialog below, the answers are not in the same order as the questions. Match the questions with their answers. When you are finished, practice the dialog.

1. Hi, how are you?
2. What's the matter?
3. Do you know what it is?
4. Are you running a fever?
5. You should probably get some rest.

a. No, no fever. I'm just not up to par.
b. Yeah, you're right. I'll get over it faster if I rest.
c. I think I'm coming down with something.
d. No, but there's something going around.
e. I'm a little under the weather.

Focus on form

A *Sentence completion*

Use these pairs of words to complete the sentences below.

back, feet	bill, health	fighting, lives	under, weather
bags, eyes	down, flu	stress, out	upsets, stomach

1. "How's your mom feeling?" "Not too good. I think she's coming down with the flu."
2. I'm sorry I couldn't make it to your party. I was ________ the ________.
3. Claudia wasn't sure the doctor would let her travel, but he gave her a clean ________ of ________.
4. Some of these kids are literally ________ for their ________.
5. He looked really tired. He had big ________ under his ________.
6. You'll be ________ on your ________ in no time!
7. Don't let these exams ________ you ________.
8. When he eats rich food, it ________ his ________.

B *Correct or incorrect?*

Are these sentences correct? Some have an extra word. Put a check (✔) in the box if the sentence is correct. Put an ✘ in the box and circle the extra word if it is wrong.

1. I think there's a bug going on around. ☒
2. I'm worn out. I've been fighting off a cold all week. ☐
3. He's running up a high fever. ☐
4. A vacation will do you a world of good. ☐
5. He's not feeling up to the par. ☐
6. It's good to see you're on the mend. ☐
7. It takes a week to get on over this flu. ☐
8. I love ice cream, but it doesn't agree with me. ☐

Focus on use

A *Formality*

Rewrite this letter from Chris to his friend Sue. Make it sound more natural by replacing the words in blue with idioms from the box. You may need to change some of the forms.

back on your feet	fight something off	stress you out	wear you out
do you a world of good	get over (something)	under the weather	

Dear Sue,

Sorry I haven't written. I was feeling unwell (1) ______________. I think I was resisting (2) ______________ a cold. Work was making me feel nervous and unhappy (3) ______________, and I think it was probably making me tired (4) ______________.

The good news is that I spent a week in the mountains. The fresh air made me feel much healthier and happier (5) ______________. I recovered from (6) ______________ my mystery illness and am feeling great (7) ______________ again.

I hope you're well and happy. I'll write again soon.

Best wishes,

Chris

B *Over to you*

Some people believe that forms of alternative medicine, like acupuncture or herbal medicine, are very effective. What do you think? Why?

Now write

Write a few words of advice for each of these people.

1. I've been working too hard and feel stressed out all the time.
2. I'm really tired when I go to bed, but then after an hour I wake up. I get up in the morning feeling completely worn out.
3. I don't know why, but every time there's something going around, I come down with it.

Unit 8

Home and family

Dear Mom and Dad,

Greetings from Australia!

You were right about Uncle Jack and Aunt Mary – we'd never met, but they made me **feel** right **at home**, and now I've really **settled in** to their beautiful house.

They've **put down** strong **roots** here in town and are well liked. Aunt Mary **wears the pants in the family**, and she's made me very welcome. It already feels like a **home away from home**.

I could see right away that Dad and Uncle Jack are brothers. (And telling bad jokes must **run in the family**, Dad!) Uncle Jack says he can tell I'm your son. He says I'm **a chip off the old block**.

Now that their own kids have grown up and **left the nest**, I think they're a little lonely. They are really spoiling me. That's all for now.

Love, Harry

Family

- **your nearest and dearest** your family
- **blood is thicker than water** connection to family is more important than anything else
- **run in the family**, *also* **run in someone's family** to be a common quality in a particular family
- **take after someone** to be like a parent or older relative – either in character or in appearance
- **a chip off the old block** a child whose character is similar to his or her mother's or father's
- ⚠ **be born with a silver spoon in your mouth** to have opportunities or advantages because you are from a rich family
- **hand down something**, *also* **hand something down** to give something old or used to someone in your family who is younger or lives longer
- **wear the pants (in the family)** to be in control of the house or the family

Home

- **home away from home** a place where you feel as comfortable as in your own home
- **feel at home** to feel comfortable and relaxed
- **in the bosom of your family** [slightly formal] feeling safe and comfortable

Leaving home

- **leave the nest**, *also* **fly the nest** to leave your parents' home
- **pull up roots** to move away from a place where you have lived and felt comfortable

Making or being in a new home

- **settle in**, *also* **put down roots (in a place)** to live someplace new and start to feel you belong there
- **settle down** to stay in one place and start behaving in a more regular way

Focus on meaning

Concept map

Complete this concept map, using the idioms in the box.

a. a chip off the old block
b. a home away from home
c. at home
d. blood is thicker than water
e. born with a silver spoon in your mouth
f. hand down
g. in the bosom of your family
h. leave the nest
i. put down roots
j. pull up roots
k. run in the family
l. settle down
m. settle in
n. take after someone
o. wear the pants
p. nearest and dearest

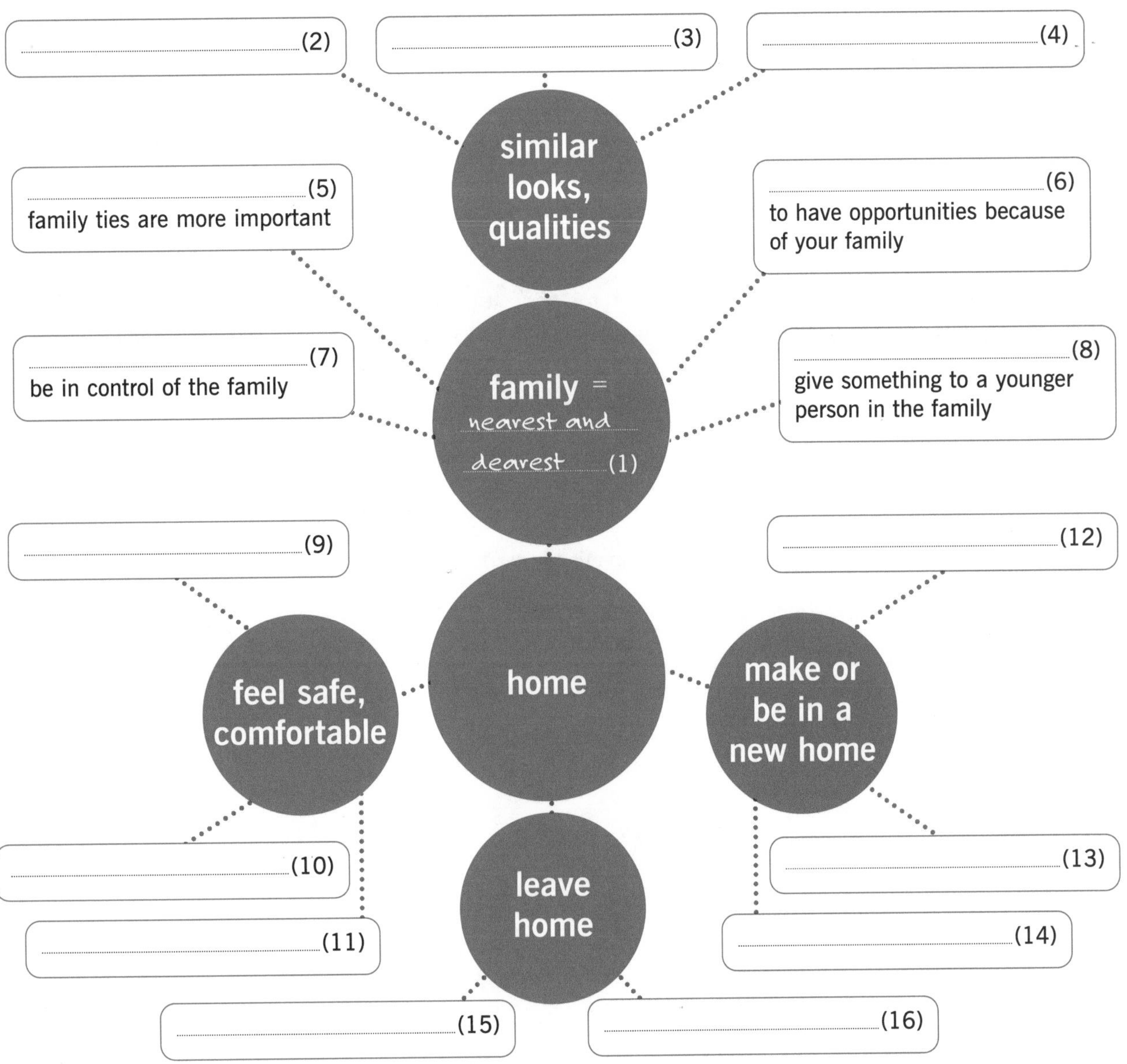

Focus on form

A *Editing*

Underline the mistakes in the sentences below. Then write the correct form of the idiom.

1. When is he going to settle under? ......settle down......
2. He's a good cook – he takes along his father. ....
3. We want to be with our dearest and nearest now. ....
4. Thanks for making us feel so in home. ....
5. Blood really is as thick as water. ....
6. She was born with a silver fork in her mouth. ....
7. We are settling on to our new home. ....
8. It was handed along to me by my mother. ....

B *Sentence completion*

Use these pairs of words to complete the sentences below. You may have to change the form of some words.

bosom, family	fly, nest	pull, roots	run, family
chip, block	home, home	put, roots	wear, pants

1. Jaime really is a ......chip...... off the old ......block...... .
2. It's hard to .... up .... after all these years.
3. That restaurant is like a .... away from .... for us now.
4. We moved here three years ago and immediately started to .... down ....
5. Good business sense seems to .... in their ....
6. The kids have all .... the .... now, and we're free to travel more.
7. Who .... the .... in this family?
8. After two years overseas, it is nice to be back in the .... of our ....

Focus on use

A *Letter from home*

Here is a letter from Harry's mother replying to his letter at the beginning of this unit. Use idioms from the unit to replace the words and phrases in blue.

Dear Harry,

Your dad and I are so glad to hear that you are beginning to feel comfortable (1) ______________ and feeling comfortable and relaxed (2) ______________ already.

Uncle Jack and Aunt Mary are fun to be with, aren't they? They were a bit wild in their younger days. In fact, we wondered whether they would ever stay in one place (3) ______________ and have kids.

They did, of course, but it's hard to believe that the kids have grown up and moved away from their parents' home (4) ______________.

You're right – telling bad jokes is a common quality in your dad's family (5) ______________. Just don't tell your dad I said that!

Lots of love,

Mom

B *Over to you*

1. *What makes you **feel at home** in a new place?*
2. *Are there any special talents, characteristics, or hobbies that **run in your family**?*

Now write

Write a short description of someone in your family, past or present. Use idioms from the unit.

Unit 9

Learning and studying

Brian: How was the interview?

Ron: It was OK, I think. I'd done my homework and read up on the company. I think they'll offer me the job.

Brian: Great. Is it something you've done before?

Ron: Not really, but I think I'll pick it up quickly. I'll need to brush up on my Spanish, because I'll be going to Latin America a lot. And I'll have to get to know the team.

Brian: It always takes a while to learn the ropes. I found out the hard way – it's a bad idea to rush. Take your time. It's better to spend more time listening than talking. I've learned that lesson!

Learning

- **at first blush** when you are first learning or thinking about something
- **learn something by rote** to learn something in a mechanical way, usually by memorizing it
- **drill something into someone** to teach a person something by repeating it often
- **learn something the hard way,** *also* **find something out the hard way** to learn through experience
- **learn a / your lesson** to learn through a bad experience
- **learn the ropes** to learn how to do a particular job or activity
- **pick up something,** *also* **pick something up** to learn about something by being in contact with it
- **soak up something,** *also* **soak something up** to learn about something quickly and easily

Studying

- **brush up on something** to quickly study about something that you have learned before
- **bone up on something** to study a subject to prepare for an exam or test
- **do your homework** to prepare for something by studying about the subject in advance
- **read up on something** to study or read a lot of information about something
- **read the fine print** to study the details of something

Focus on meaning

Paraphrasing

Rewrite these sentences by paraphrasing the idioms in blue.

1. At first blush, they seemed like the perfect neighbors.

   When we first met them, they seemed like the perfect neighbors.

2. Make sure you bone up on local history before the quiz.

3. Most of us need to brush up on our computer skills.

4. We learned our multiplication tables by rote.

5. It was clear that she had done her homework before the meeting.

6. We had the safety procedures drilled into us.

7. You can't trust the department head – I found out the hard way.

8. I've learned my lesson. I'm not going to spend more than I can afford.

9. He's been working here for only two weeks. He's still learning the ropes.

10. We're having trouble learning English, but our kids picked it up quickly.

11. It's worth reading up on the museums in the city.

12. My sister likes studying in classrooms, but I prefer to sit in sidewalk cafés and soak up the language.

Focus on form

A *Learning and studying crossword*

Complete the crossword by filling in the missing word in each idiom.

Across

1 at first .... (5)

3 learn your .... (6)

5 learn by .... (4)

6 .... up on something (4)

7 .... up something (4)

Down

1 .... up on something (5)

2 do your .... (8)

4 learn the .... (5)

B *Sentence completion*

Use the idioms in parentheses to complete the following sentences. Use the correct verb forms.

1. The importance of accuracy was ....drilled into.... them. (drill into)

2. .... in a new job can take time. (learn the ropes)

3. He never had guitar lessons. He just .... it .... (pick up)

4. Luke knows how strict speed limits are – and he .... (find out the hard way)

5. Take some time to .... each subject. (bone up on)

6. I've .... I'll never fill in another online questionnaire! (learn *your* lesson)

Focus on use

A *Dialogs*

Work with a partner. Choose one of the situations below. One person takes Part A; the other takes Part B. Create a dialog using idioms from the unit.

Situation 1: Interview

A

Your friend is worried about going to an interview for a job he or she really wants. Advise him or her about how to prepare.

B

You're really worried about an interview for a job. You have never had a job interview before and don't know what to expect. Ask your friend to tell you what you should do to get ready.

Situation 2: New job

A

You're starting a new job tomorrow, and you're worried about it. Ask for advice.

B

You work at the company. You were nervous the night before you started. Tell your friend about your experiences and suggest ways to prepare and what to expect.

B *Over to you*

Have you ever ***learned something the hard way****? What did you learn? How did you feel?*

Now write

Write a paragraph about **learning the ropes** in a new situation.

Unit 10

Money

Christine: Wow, Winnie! What happened – did you strike it rich and win the lottery or something?

Winnie: In a way, yes. After college, I taught for a while. I wanted to go back to painting, but I had to do something to bring home the bacon. Well, I found some really good artists. We set up our own Web site, and we started selling our paintings on the Internet.

Christine: Really?

Winnie: Yes, we didn't really expect to turn a profit, but we hoped to break even.

Christine: And?

Winnie: We got lots of work and made a killing.

Christine: Really?

Winnie: Yes, the customers are happy because they get their money's worth, and we're laughing all the way to the bank.

Christine: Great. You can take me to lunch.

Winnie: I'd love to! Where do you want to go? Money is no object.

Earning or making money

- **break even** to earn, or make, as much money as you spend
- **turn a profit** to earn, or make, more money than you spend
- **bring home the bacon** to earn money to live on
- **pull down (an amount of money)** to earn a lot of money
- **clean up,** *also* **make a killing** *or* **strike it rich** to make a lot of money
- **laughing all the way to the bank** making a lot of money easily

Having money

- **in the money** to have (or suddenly get) a lot of money
- **money talks** money is powerful

Spending money

- **get your money's worth** to get good value for the money you spend
- **throw good money after bad** to continue to spend money on something that is failing
- **throw money at something** (like a project) to try to solve problems by just spending a lot of money on something
- **money is no object** the cost of something is not important
- **(something costs) an arm and a leg** something is very expensive

Focus on meaning

A *Sentence completion*

Use the idioms from the box to complete the following sentences. You may have to change the form of some words.

break even	get your money's worth	throw good money after bad
bring home the bacon	money is no object	turn a profit

1. In the restaurant business, they say you can expect to wait five years before you

   ......turn a profit...... .

2. Don't leave before the end of the concert. Stay until the end and .... !
3. Don't spend another dime on it – you're just ....
4. When it comes to our kids' education, ...
5. We don't expect to make money right away. We would like to

   .... , though.

6. It's a good, steady job and it helps me ....

B *Odd one out*

Look at the idioms in 1–5 below. Two of the idioms have similar meanings, and one is different. Circle the idiom that does not belong.

1. a. make a killing
   b. strike it rich
   c. an arm and a leg
2. a. throw money at something
   b. throw good money after bad
   c. break even
3. a. clean up
   b. throw good money after bad
   c. make a killing
4. a. in the money
   b. laughing all the way to the bank
   c. money talks
5. a. an arm and a leg
   b. pull down (money)
   c. bring home the bacon

Focus on form

A *Correct or incorrect?*

Are these sentences correct? Put a check (✔) in the box if the sentence is correct. Put an ✘ in the box and correct the idiom if it is wrong.

1. We didn't make any money, but we broke even. ☑ ....
2. When things started to go wrong, he just threw money on it. ☐ ....
3. She's pulling up about $80,000 a year. ☐ ....
4. Congratulations! You've struck it rich! ☐ ....
5. Their company was the first one to turn on a profit. ☐ ....
6. Order whatever you want. Money is no object. ☐ ....

B *Prepositions and adverbs*

Use the prepositions and adverbs in the box to complete the sentences.

after	at	down	even	in	to	up

1. When the rain started, the guys selling umbrellas really cleaned ....up.... .
2. A college graduate cannot expect to pull .... a good salary automatically.
3. They've been throwing money .... that project for years.
4. You're not just going to throw good money .... bad, are you?
5. We found some rare books in the attic, and now we're .... the money.
6. It's great! We're laughing all the way .... the bank.

Focus on use

A *Formality*

Make this ad for a salesperson sound more natural by replacing the phrases in blue with idioms from the unit.

Are you interested in **making as much money as you spend**

(1) ....?

Or possibly even **making more than you spend**

(2) ....?

Then we don't want to hear from you.

We want to hear from people who are genuinely interested in

making a lot of money (3) ....

Don't get us wrong – we want our customers to **get good value for the money they spend (4)** ...., and we don't want them to have to pay **very high prices (5)** .... for our products.

But we do want them to buy, and we want you to sell, sell, sell!

Give us a call today . . .

B *Over to you*

In a social conversation in your culture, is it polite or impolite to ask direct questions about a person's financial situation? Which idioms in this unit would be acceptable in your culture?

Now write

In American English the proverb "A penny saved is a penny earned" reflects the social value that people should save money instead of spending it. Write about an idiom or a proverb about money in your language. What social values does the phrase reflect? Do you think those values are also important in American culture? Why or why not?

Unit 11

Negotiations and decisions

Mark: Now, we've come to the table to try to hammer out an agreement about the rock concert in the park this summer.

I know we all have very strong views about this, but I think that, with some give and take on both sides, we'll reach an agreement. Maria, as the concert organizer, will you start, please?

Maria: OK. I'll put our cards on the table. We want to hold a five-day concert in the park, and we want to allow campers to stay overnight in the parking lot.

Alice: The mayor's office will permit a two-day concert, against our better judgment, but we draw the line at camping in the parking lot!

Maria: Well, we're willing to meet you halfway. We can move the camping out of town if we can hold a four-day concert.

Mark: All right, let's split the difference – what about a long weekend?

Maria: That sounds good to us. Now what about dates?

Mark: Well, let's take a look at the calendar . . .

Negotiating

- **come to the table** to meet to discuss how to solve a problem or reach an agreement
- **give and take** the exchange of some of what you want for some of what someone else wants
- **meet someone halfway,** *also* **split the difference** not the best decision you believe you could make
- **hammer something out,** *also* **hammer out something** to create an agreeable solution
- **put your cards on the table,** *also* **tip your hand** *or* **show your hand** to explain what you think and what you want
- **up the ante,** *also* **raise the ante** to increase demands, risk, or cost so that you can get more from a situation

Making decisions

- **between a rock and a hard place** to be in a difficult position and have only unpleasant choices
- **on the fence** undecided
- **draw the line at doing something** to decide you will not do something
- **against your better judgment** [slightly formal] not the best decision you believe you could make
- **take the plunge** to decide to do something that is difficult or risky
- **seal someone's / something's fate** [slightly formal] to decide that something, usually negative, will happen to someone or something

Focus on meaning

Concept map

Complete this concept map, using the idioms in the box.

a. against your better judgment
b. between a rock and a hard place
c. come to the table
d. draw the line at doing something
e. give and take
f. hammer something out
g. meet someone halfway
h. on the fence
i. put your cards on the table
j. seal someone's / something's fate
k. split the difference
l. take the plunge
m. show *or* tip your hand
n. up the ante *or* raise the ante

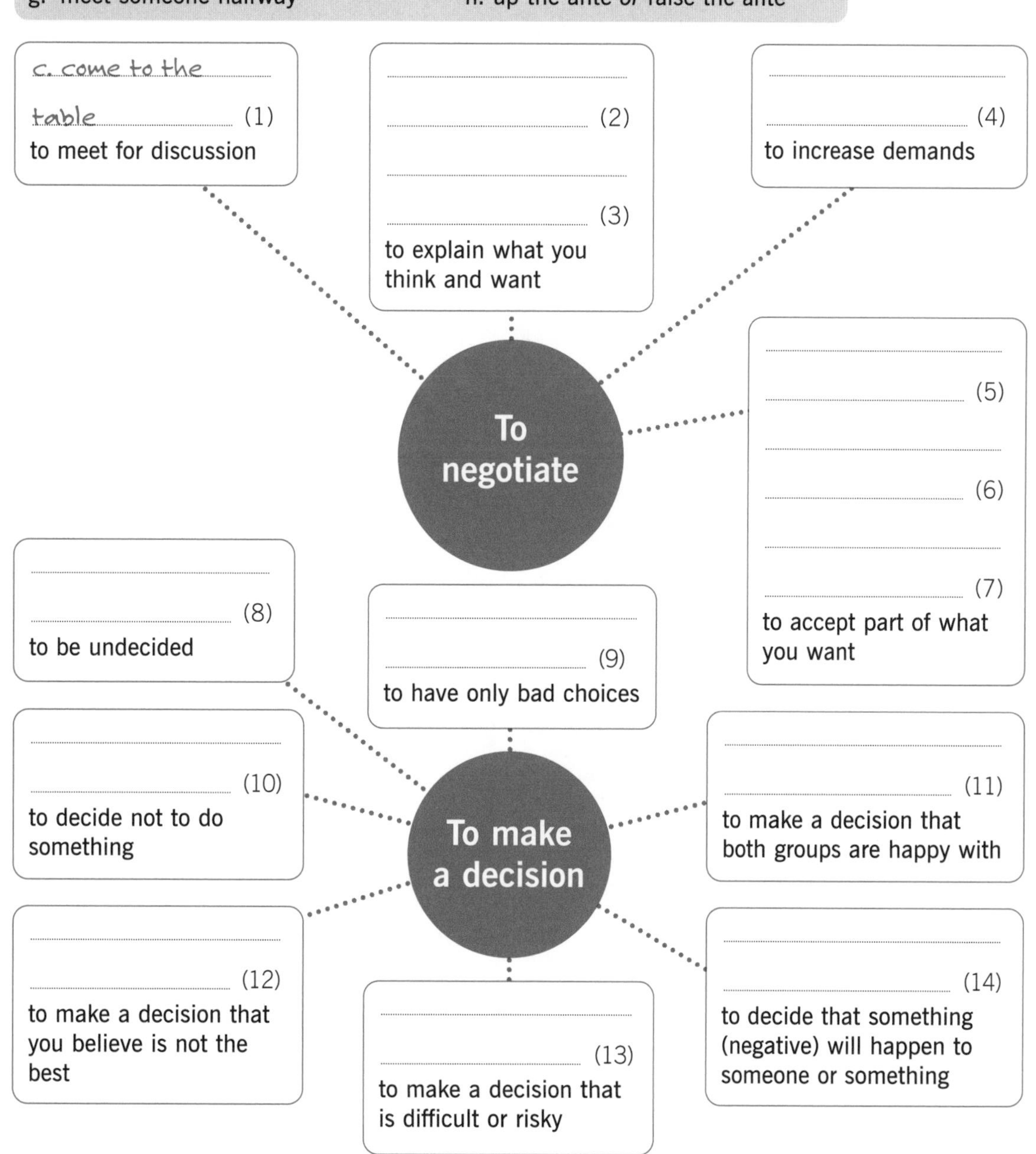

Focus on form

A *Scrambled story*

Correct the text by putting the lines in the correct order. The first and last lines are done for you.

1 The two groups finally decided to **come to the**

...... **take,** they decided that they would **take**

...... **each other halfway,** but eventually, after a lot of **give and**

...... **table** to discuss the issue and to **hammer out**

...... **their cards on the table.** At first, they weren't willing to **meet**

...... **a solution** they'd both be happy with. They **put**

7 **the plunge** and try something new.

B *Correct or incorrect?*

Are these sentences correct? Put a check (✔) in the box if the sentence is correct. Put an ✘ in the box and correct the idiom if it is wrong.

1. This is terrible. We're between a hard rock and a place. ☒ We're between a rock and a hard place.
2. Students are welcome to use the Internet for research, but we draw the line at chat rooms. ☐ ......
3. Let's meet the difference and set the price at $150. ☐ ......
4. His decision to drop out of college sealed his fate. ☐ ......
5. OK, you can go, but it's against the better judgment. ☐ ......
6. The employees raised the ante and said they would strike. ☐ ......
7. Stop beating along the bush. ☐ ......

Focus on use

A *Negotiation role play*

Work with a partner. One person takes Part A, on page 163; the other takes Part B, on page 164. Think about your situation and plan how you can get what you want, or most of what you want. Use idioms from the unit as you try to reach an agreement.

The situation: A large company, EcoGolf, wants to build a big hotel and golf course in Loon Lake, a small town on a beautiful lake.

The good points about a hotel and a golf course in the town:

- 50–60 new jobs
- more tourists spending money in local businesses
- better facilities (golf course, swimming pool, gym) for the people who live in the town

The bad points about the hotel and golf course:

- an increase in road traffic
- possible problems with power supply, water, etc.
- possible pollution in the lake

Student A: Turn to the role card on p. 163.
Student B: Turn to the role card on p. 164.

B *Over to you*

Some of the idioms in this unit – ***show your hand, put your cards on the table, up the ante*** *– come from card games.*

Can you think of any negotiating idioms in your language that come from games?

Now write

Write about a difficult decision that you had to make. Use idioms from the unit.

Unit 12

Personality and character

Lori: I met your friend John last night. He's got a chip on his shoulder, hasn't he?

Julia: He comes across like that at first, but then you realize he's shy. Actually, he is the salt of the earth.

Lori: Really? He didn't seem very nice at all.

Julia: Believe me, John has a heart of gold, and he's as kind as they come.

Lori: He barely talked to anybody and stood there looking angry.

Julia: He's a man of few words, that's true. But he doesn't have a nasty bone in his body.

Positive character idioms

- **(have a) heart of gold** to have a kind and generous character. The opposite is **a heart of stone.**
- **at peace with yourself** to feel calm and relaxed about your life
- **at your best** showing your best characteristics
- **blessed with something** to have that (positive) quality
- **salt of the earth** good, ordinary people
- **a man (or person) of few words** a person who does not talk unnecessarily

Negative character idioms

- **(have) a chip on your shoulder** to get angry or upset easily because you feel you have been treated unfairly
- ⚠ **full of yourself** thinking that you are important, in a way that annoys other people

Character idioms that can be negative, positive, or neutral

- **not have a *friendly* / *honest* / *selfish* bone in your body** to not be friendly, honest, selfish,
- **as *friendly* / *honest* / *selfish* as they come** extremely friendly, honest, selfish, etc.
- **(have) a thick skin** to not be sensitive to personal criticism
- **(something that is) in your blood** a central part of your character
- **be yourself** to behave in a way that is natural to you
- **come across (as something)** to seem to have a particular attitude or character

Focus on meaning

A *Sentence completion*

Use idioms from the box to complete the following sentences. You may have to change the form of some words.

at peace with (yourself)	come across as	a heart of stone
at your best	(have) a thick skin	in your blood
blessed with	have a *[type of]* bone in your body	

1. Their story is very sad. You'd have to have a heart of stone not to be moved by it.
2. She's a great teacher – she's ________ patience and understanding.
3. How can you call him dishonest? He doesn't ________.
4. She was an angry young woman, but now that she's older, she's ________.
5. He ________ efficient at first, but he's really disorganized.
6. I was nervous and definitely not ________ when I gave the presentation.
7. In the music business you have to ________ to survive.
8. I love this game. It's ________. My parents were golfers too.

B *Correct or incorrect?*

Below each numbered sentence is a restatement of it. Put a check (✔) in the box if the restatement is correct. If it is incorrect, put an ✘ in the box and correct it.

1. Helen and Brian are the salt of the earth. ☒ Helen and Brian are good and ordinary people.
   Helen and Brian are fun-loving people.
2. Linda is as honest as they come. ☐ ________
   Linda is honest.
3. He was a man of few words ☐ ________
   He was not a good speaker.
4. He walks around as if he has a chip on his shoulder. ☐ ________
   He acts like a strong, friendly person.
5. Ellie has a heart of gold. ☐ ________
   Ellie is a kind, generous person.
6. I'd like him if he weren't so full of himself. ☐ ________
   I don't like him because he's dishonest.

Focus on form

A *Sentence transformation*

Rewrite these sentences, using the idioms in parentheses.

1. Margot has unlimited energy and enthusiasm. (blessed with)

   Margot is blessed with unlimited energy and enthusiasm.

2. Murat seems lazy. (come across as)

3. Karla is completely trustworthy. (as _____ as they come)

4. He doesn't have many friends because he thinks he's so important. (full of yourself)

5. He was more calm and relaxed about his life as he got older. (at peace with yourself)

B *Sentence completion*

Make complete sentences using the words in the order given. You may have to change the form of some words.

1. David / successful / business / because / heart of stone.

   David is successful in business because he has a heart of stone.

2. Katya / unkind / bone in (your) body.

3. Go / bed / early / so / you / be / at (your) best / interview / tomorrow.

4. Barry / have / chip on (your) shoulder.

5. Farmers / be / salt of the earth.

6. Penny / have / thick skin.

Focus on use

A *Dialog completion*

You are a publicist for Al Wright, a movie star. A journalist is waiting to interview Al. Al has kept the journalist waiting for over an hour. Complete the dialog by trying to convince the journalist that Al is a nice, thoughtful person. Use at least two idioms from the unit.

Journalist: Does he always keep people waiting like this?

He must be pretty full of himself!

You: Not at all. (1) ....

Journalist: I've heard that he has a chip on his shoulder

because he never got a chance to finish college.

You: (2) ....

Journalist: He certainly comes across as being selfish.

You: (3) ....

B *Over to you*

Can you think of an idiom or a phrase in your own language that means the same as these idioms?

salt of the earth

a chip on your shoulder

not have [***a type of***] bone in your body

Now write

Think of someone you admire. Describe his or her personality and explain why you admire that person.

Unit 13

Problems and solutions

Luis: How's the project going?

Gladys: Well, we've hit a snag.

Luis: What's the problem?

Gladys: The programmers haven't been paid. They're in dire straits, financially. Without the software, we'll be up the creek.

Luis: What'll we do?

Gladys: Well, I wish we could just wave a magic wand and get the money we need. Come to my office this afternoon, and bring John and Sarah. We'll put our heads together, think outside the box, and try to come up with a solution.

Problems

- **hit a snag** to experience a difficulty
- **a tough nut (to crack),** *also* **a hard nut (to crack)** a difficult problem to solve
- ⚠ **a thorn in the side** something or someone that is continually causing problems

Difficult situations

- **in a bind** forced to deal with a difficult situation
- **in a tight spot** in a difficult situation
- **in dire straits** in extreme danger or difficulty
- **up the creek** in an extremely difficult situation
- **with your back against the wall** in a serious situation with few ways to react to it
- **when the chips are down** when you are in a difficult or dangerous situation

Trying to solve problems

- **put your heads together** to share ideas in trying to solve a problem
- **puzzle over something** to give a lot of attention and thought to something
- **think outside the box** to solve problems creatively

Solving problems

- **paper over something,** *also* **paper something over** to solve a problem temporarily
- **come up with something** to find, think of, or develop a solution
- **save the day** do something to solve a serious problem
- **wave a magic wand** solve a difficult problem with no effort
- **puzzle something out** to study something in order to understand it

Focus on meaning

A *Correct or Incorrect?*

Below each numbered sentence is a restatement of it. Put a check (✔) in the box if the restatement is correct. If it is incorrect, put an ✘ in the box and correct it.

1. The team has hit a snag. ☒ The team has a problem.
   The team isn't very good.
2. Jay is very good at thinking outside the box. ☐ ____________
   Jay is a creative thinker.
3. I wish I could just wave a magic wand and make everything OK. ☐ ____________
   I wish I could solve this problem temporarily.
4. They papered over the cracks and hoped no one would notice. ☐ ____________
   They solved the problem temporarily.
5. College students are often in dire financial straits. ☐ ____________
   College students often have serious money problems.
6. Kate has been a real thorn in our side. ☐ ____________
   Kate is a creative thinker.

B *Odd one out*

Look at the idioms in 1–5 below. Two of the idioms have similar meanings, and one is different. Circle the idiom that does not belong.

1. a. up the creek
   b. a thorn in the side (circled)
   c. in dire straits
2. a. come up with something
   b. save the day
   c. hit a snag
3. a. put your heads together
   b. puzzle something out
   c. hit a snag
4. a. wave a magic wand
   b. a tough nut to crack
   c. save the day
5. a. when the chips are down
   b. with your back against the wall
   c. wave a magic wand
6. a. paper over something
   b. in a bind
   c. in a tight spot

Focus on form

A *Prepositions and adverbs*

Use the prepositions and adverbs in the box to complete the sentences. You may need to use some of them more than once.

against	down	in	outside	over	up	with

1. I'll take the report home and puzzle over it this weekend.
2. He's a great friend when the chips are ________.
3. We're trying to come ________ ________ a win-win solution.
4. I think we're ________ the creek this time!
5. This shop has never made money – it's always been a thorn ________ my side.
6. Forget what you learned at school. Now it's time to think ________ the box.
7. I don't know what to do. Our backs are really ________ the wall!
8. They're ________ a tight spot and need our help.

B *Key words*

Using the key words in parentheses, put the idioms into these sentences. Use the correct verb forms. Add any needed words to make the sentences correct.

1. Let's put our heads together and see what we can do. (put/heads/together)
2. You're wonderful. You ________________! (save/day)
3. We knew we didn't have a solution. We were just ________________ the cracks. (paper/over)
4. They are really good at ________________. (think/outside/box)
5. Do you think you can just ________________ and expect everything to be all right? (wave/magic/wand)
6. Don't worry. We've been ________________ before. We'll be OK. (dire/straits)

Focus on use

A *Formality*

*Rewrite this advertisement to make it sound more natural. Replace the words in **bold** with idioms from the unit*

Balancing a job, college, and a social life can be a **difficult problem to solve** (1) ______________. Sometimes, especially when you are **in a difficult situation** (2) ______________ financially, you may feel that **your situation is really serious and that there is not much you can do** (3) ______________.

But don't worry! *Magic Wand Finance* is here to **solve all your problems** (4) ______________! And we won't just **temporarily solve** (5) ______________ your problems. We'll **think of** (6) ______________ effective, long-term solutions to help you do all the things you want to do.

Visit our Web site or call toll-free …

B *Over to you*

1. *Have you ever had to think outside the box to solve a difficult problem? Are you good at that kind of problem solving, or do you know someone who is?*
2. *What would you say if you were working on a problem and the other members of the team just wanted to paper over the cracks?*

Now write

Write about **a thorn in the side** that you or someone you know has experienced.

Unit 14 Relationships

Mom: Today is Grandma and Grandpa's fiftieth wedding anniversary.

Dave: Wow, they go back a long way.

Mom: Yes, they do. They met in high school. But it wasn't exactly love at first sight. When they first met, they didn't hit it off at all. Grandma says she didn't think they had anything in common. She tried to keep Grandpa at arm's length.

Then, when she turned eighteen, he just swept her off her feet and she realized she'd fallen in love.

Friendship

- **go back a long way** to know someone for a long time
- **hit it off** to like each other immediately
- **have something in common (with someone)** to have similar interests or characteristics
- **build bridges** to try to create relationships
- **mend (your) fences** to try to repair relationships
- **keep someone at arm's length** to try to avoid becoming connected or friendly with someone
- **part company (with someone)** to end a relationship with someone

Romance

- **fall in love (with someone)** *also* **lose your heart (to someone)** to begin to love someone
- **love at first sight** an immediate attraction when you meet someone for the first time
- **sweep someone off his / her feet** to cause someone to love you suddenly and completely
- **(be) head over heels (in love),** *also* **to have got it bad** to be very much in love
- **hung up on someone** to be foolishly in love with that person
- **on the rocks** likely to fail. Used in speaking about relationships.

Focus on meaning

Super crossword

Complete the crossword by filling in the missing word in each idiom.

Across

4 to try to create relationships: .... bridges (5)

5 to cause someone to fall in love with you: .... someone off his / her feet (5)

7 likely to fail: on the .... (5)

9 to like someone immediately: .... it off (3)

10 to repair relationships: .... fences (4)

11 to begin to love someone: .... in love (4)

12 foolishly in love: .... up on (4)

Down

1 to be very much in love: got it .... (3)

2 to fall in love: .... your heart (4)

3 to avoid becoming connected with someone: .... someone at arm's length (4)

4 to know someone a long time: go .... a long way (4)

6 to end a relationship: .... company (4)

8 to have similar interests or characteristics: to have something in .... (6)

9 to be very much in love: head over .... (5)

11 an immediate attraction: love at .... sight (5)

Focus on form

A *What's wrong with these sentences?*

Find and correct the mistake in each sentence.

1. We just didn't it hit off. .... We just didn't hit it off.
2. We need to build fences between divisions. ....
3. Try to meet him at arm's length. ....
4. We go behind a long way. ....
5. It's obvious that their marriage is in the rocks. ....
6. Is it too late to mend a fence with your ex-husband? ....
7. We knew it was time to part our company. ....
8. Let's fall on love! ....
9. I lost my hearts. ....

B *Pronunciation love poem*

Use idioms from the box to complete the poem.

got it bad	hung up on	love at first sight
head over heels	in common	swept off your feet

Do you know how it feels
To be head over heels (1)?
The first time you meet
You're .... (2).

You spend years alone
Think you're fine on your own.
Then on one magic night
It's .... (3).

Then you're .... (4) someone
Who you're hoping is fun.
You don't know if you've got
Things .... (5) or not.

But now you're not sad
Because you've .... (6),
And you're wishing, my friend,
That this love will not end.

Focus on use

A *What's your advice?*

You write an advice column in a newspaper. Using some of the idioms in the unit, create a short paragraph of advice to each writer.

Ask *In the Know*

1. Dear *ITK*,
Several years ago I got really mad at my sister. I stopped talking to her. She got my e-mail address and has started writing to me regularly. She apologized for everything. Should I reply to her e-mails or continue to keep her at arm's length?

Karen T.

2. Dear *ITK*,
I'm worried about my partner. He doesn't talk to me anymore. We don't seem to have any fun anymore. Should I try to build bridges?

Chris L.

3. Dear *ITK*,
An old friend of mine recently got in touch. I hadn't heard from him in years. He wants me to go into business with him. He has not had much luck. I have the money, and we do go back a long way. What do you think I should do?

Max R.

4. Dear *ITK*,
I met someone at a New Year's Eve party. We really hit it off. We've got a lot in common. I'm head over heels in love and I think she is, too, but I'm not sure. I'm nervous about telling her. Should I take a chance and tell her how I feel?

Terry N.

B *Over to you*

Do you believe in ***love at first sight****? Why or why not?*

Now write

Write a short paragraph about a romance or a friendship. Use at least three idioms from the unit.

Unit 15

Time

Beth: What are you doing at the moment?

Wendy: I'm trying to finish my paper. I didn't do any work during the vacation, so I'm trying to make up for lost time now.

Beth: How about seeing a movie?

Wendy: I can't. I'm working day and night trying to finish this thing.

Beth: You need to take a break every now and then.

Wendy: Thursday is the drop-dead date. I have to finish it.

Happening now

- **at the moment** now
- **for the time being** at this time
- **the here and now** the present

Happening later

- **down the line,** *also* **down the road** [especially spoken] in the future
- **in the fullness of time** [slightly formal] after enough time passes
- **drop-dead date** a time by which something must be done

The present affected by the past

- **make up for lost time** to do things you were not able to do before
- **turn back the clock,** *also* **turn the clock back** to make things as they were in the past

Frequency

- **around the clock** continuously, all day and all night
- **day and night,** *also* **night and day** all the time
- **every now and then** sometimes
- **once in a blue moon** almost never, rarely

Periods or amounts of time

- **all along** the whole time
- **for the long haul** for a long period of time
- **in the long run,** *also* **in the long term** finally
- **in a (New York) minute,** *also* **in a heartbeat** in a very short time, quickly
- **in the short run,** *also* **in the short term** for a short period

Focus on meaning

A *Time line*

Put the idioms in the box onto the time line.

at the moment	drop-dead date	in the fullness of time	the here and now
down the line	for the time being	make up for lost time	turn back the clock

Idioms to describe:

The past affecting the present	The present (now)	The future
turn back the clock	....	....
....	....	....
	....	....

B *Time scale*

Put the idioms in the box onto the scale.

around the clock	once in a blue moon	day and night	(every) now and then

Always (100%)	Sometimes (50%)	Rarely (15% – 0%)
1 day and night	2	3 ....
....		

C *Correct or incorrect?*

Below each numbered sentence is a restatement of it. Put a check (✔) in the box if the restatement is correct. If it is incorrect, put an ✘ in the box and correct it.

1. He's seriously ill and needs care around the clock. ☒ He cannot take care of himself.
   He can take care of himself.
2. She could change her mind in a New York minute. ☐ ....
   She might change her mind very quickly.
3. He knew about the surprise party all along. ☐ ....
   The party was not a surprise to him.
4. They are hoping for big sales in the long run. ☐ ....
   They expect big sales in the near future.
5. They are hoping for big sales in the short run. ☐ ....
   They expect big sales in the near future.
6. We are in this project for the long haul. ☐ ....
   We plan to be involved in this project for many years.

Focus on form

A *Prepositions and adverbs*

Use the prepositions and adverbs in the box to complete the sentences. You may need to use some of them more than once.

around	at	back	for	in	up

1. They hadn't seen each other in years, so they stayed up all night talking and trying to make ___up___ ___for___ lost time.
2. We aren't expecting to make a profit ________ the short term.
3. The police are watching the house ________ the clock.
4. I'm sorry, she's not at her desk ________ the moment. Can I take a message?
5. Don't get too much sun. It's not good for your skin ________ the long run.
6. Once ________ a blue moon, we order a pizza to be delivered.
7. Don't you wish we could just turn ________ the clock?

B *Sentence transformation*

Rewrite these sentences, using the idioms in parentheses.

1. The rescue team has been working all the time. (day and night)

   The rescue team has been working day and night.

2. This assignment has to be in by June 2. (drop-dead date)

   ____

3. He has been dishonest the whole time. (all along)

   ____

4. We're happy living here at this time. (for the time being)

   ____

5. Remember to e-mail us sometimes! (every now and then)

   ____

6. They advised us to forget about the past and to concentrate on the present. (here and now)

   ____

7. I'd quit this job and take that one very quickly if they offered it to me. (in a heartbeat)

   ____

Focus on use

A *Formality*

Rewrite this e-mail from Joe to his friend Pete. Make it sound more natural by replacing the words in **bold** *with idioms from the unit.*

New Message

To: Pete

From: Joe

Subject: Busy times

Sorry I haven't written lately. I've been really busy since I got here. We've been working **all the time** (1)........................ to see all the patients, but there aren't many doctors on the staff and some of the patients are very ill and need care **continuously** (2)........................ .

The clinic is quiet **now** (3)........................ .

I'm really glad I came. I am slowly learning the language and am ready to stay **for a long period of time** (4)........................ .

It is really exciting, and I think that I will make a difference **after enough time passes** (5)........................ .

We don't have much of a social life. We see people from the city **very rarely** (6) .... I like it here, though, and I would make the decision to come here again **very quickly** (7)........................ .

I hope you're OK. Take care of yourself.

B *Over to you*

Have you ever wished you could **turn back the clock** *for any reason? Think of one point in your life when you could have done something differently. How would it have changed things?*

Now write

Write a short paragraph about a period when you tried to **make up for lost time**.

Unit 16

Travel

Harold: How do you like being home?

Kevin: To tell you the truth, I'm beginning to get itchy feet already.

Harold: Really? You just got back! You were on the road for a long time.

Kevin: I know. But I feel like getting away from it all again.

Harold: Sometimes I wish I could hit the road and go somewhere off the beaten track.

Kevin: Well, if you can tear yourself away from all this, why don't you come with me?

Harold: Are you serious?

Kevin: I'm completely serious. But I travel light. No laptops, no cell phones – just a backpack and a sleeping bag.

Harold: Excellent! When do we leave?

Traveling

- **(have) itchy feet** to want to travel
- **hit the road** to begin traveling away from home
- **get away from it all** to go somewhere that is completely different
- **on the go** while traveling
- **on the road** traveling to different places
- **lay over** to stop in a place while you are traveling
- **off the beaten track** not known by many people
- **set off,** *also* **set out** to start going somewhere
- **travel light** to take very few things with you when you go on a trip

Leaving

- **duck out (of somewhere)** to leave a place quickly and without being noticed
- **show someone the door** to make someone leave
- **see someone off,** *also* **see off someone** to go with a person to the place where he or she begins a trip
- **slip out** to leave quietly and quickly
- ⚠ **take a walk,** *also* **take a hike** [rude when addressed to someone else] to leave
- **tear yourself away (from someone / something)** to force yourself to leave someone or someplace

Focus on meaning

A *Odd one out*

Look at the idioms in 1–5 below. Two of the idioms have similar meanings, and one is different. Circle the idiom that does not belong.

1. a. duck out
   b. set off (circled)
   c. slip out
2. a. hit the road
   b. set off
   c. see someone off
3. a. show someone the door
   b. on the go
   c. on the road
4. a. take a walk
   b. take a hike
   c. lay over
5. a. go off the beaten track
   b. get away from it all
   c. see someone off

B *Sentence completion*

Use idioms from the box to complete the following sentences. You may have to change the form of some words.

get away from it all	off the beaten track	tear yourself away
(get) itchy feet	set off	travel light
hit the road		

1. Winter is coming, and a lot of us will get itchy feet.
2. Why don't you find somewhere ______ where you can really ______?
3. Be realistic. Do you really think you can ______ from the city and ______?
4. He never checks in his bag at airports, so he has to ______.
5. What time do you want to ______ in the morning?

Focus on form

A *Travel and going places crossword*

Complete the crossword by filling in the missing word in each idiom.

Across

3 see someone ....

4 off the .... track

7 .... out

8 .... feet

10 lay ....

11 .... yourself away

Down

1 travel ....

2 take a ....

3 .... the go

5 get .... from it all

6 .... off

7 show someone the ....

9 .... the road

B *Scrambled story*

Correct the text by putting the lines in the correct order. The first and last lines are done for you.

1	Last semester, when the weather started to get cold, I **got itchy**
......	**beaten track**. Now I'm back. It was a good trip. I had to **tear myself**
......	**away from it all** and take time to think about things. I **slipped**
......	**feet** and decided that it was time for a change. I wanted to **get**
......	**the road**. I wasn't sure where I was going – just someplace **off the**
......	**out** of the dorm early one morning. I didn't know how long I'd be **on**
7	**away from** beach life, but I'll get back there someday.

Focus on use

A *Formality*

Rewrite this dialog to make it sound more natural. Replace the words in blue with idioms from the box. You will need to change some of the forms.

show someone the door	slip out	take a hike	tear yourself away

Alice: My son was out all night. He must have left quietly and quickly (1) ____________. I didn't even hear him leave.

Mary: Where was he all night?

Alice: Some club. He said the music was so good he had to force himself to leave (2) ____________!

Mary: What did you do?

Alice: I threw his stuff out the window and made him leave (3) ____________! I told him to leave (4) ____________ and never come back!

B *Over to you*

1. *What advice would you give to someone who* ***has itchy feet****?*
2. *Have you ever been to a place you had to* ***tear yourself away from****? Where was it?*
3. *Some people say that "you can never go back" to a place you've left. What do you think that means? Do you agree?*

Now write

Write a paragraph describing the ideal place for you to **get away from it all**. Would it be someplace **off the beaten track** or a popular tourist spot?

Unit 17 Understanding

Eric: What are you doing?

Ellen: I'm trying to get my head around this assignment. I can't seem to make heads or tails out of it. I've just read it for the tenth time, and I'm none the wiser.

Eric: What's the problem? Didn't your teacher explain it in class?

Ellen: Well, she did, but I was half asleep and kept losing the thread.

Eric: Let me see it. I took that class last year. Maybe I can get a handle on it . . . OK, I think I get the picture. You're supposed to talk to four different people and ask them these questions.

Understanding something

- **connect the dots** to understand how different ideas or situations are related
- **get a fix on something,** *also* **get a handle on something** to understand something
- **get the drift,** *also* **catch the drift** to understand the general idea of something
- **get the picture** to understand a situation
- **get your head around something,** *also* **get your mind around something** to understand something difficult
- **put two and two together** to understand something by using information you have
- **come to grips with something** to try to understand and deal with a problem or a situation

Not understanding something

- **be none the wiser,** *also* **not be (any) the wiser** *or* **not make heads or tails (out) of something** to be unable to understand something
- **"Go figure,"** *also* **"How's that?"** said about something that you don't understand
- ⚠ **slow on the uptake** not able to understand something quickly
- **beyond me,** *also* **it's beyond me** impossible to understand
- **lose the thread (of something)** to be unable to understand something because you are not paying attention
- **go over someone's head** to not be understood by someone
- **miss the point** to fail to understand the important parts of something

Focus on meaning

A *Grouping*

Put the idioms in the box into the correct group.

a. be none the wiser
b. come to grips with something
c. connect the dots
d. get a fix on something
e. get the drift
f. get the picture
g. get your head around something
h. "Go figure."
i. something goes over someone's head
j. "How's that?"
k. lose the thread (of something)
l. not make heads or tails (out) of something
m. miss the point
n. put two and two together
o. something is beyond me, it's beyond me
p. slow on the uptake

Understand

b. come to grips with something
______
______
______
______
______
______

Not understand

______
______
______
______
______
______
______
______
______

B *Odd one out*

Look at the idioms in 1–5 below. Two of the idioms have similar meanings, and one is different. Circle the idiom that does not belong.

1. a. get the picture
   b. "How's that?"
   c. "Go figure."

2. a. get the picture
   b. connect the dots
   c. lose the thread

3. a. be none the wiser
   b. not make heads or tails of something
   c. connect the dots

4. a. get your head around something
   b. come to grips with something
   c. goes over someone's head

5. a. lose the thread
   b. miss the point
   c. get the drift

Focus on form

A *Prepositions*

Use the prepositions in the box to complete the sentences. You will need to use one preposition more than once.

around	beyond	on	out	over	with

1. Sometimes I'm a little slow ___on___ the uptake.
2. "Why did they give him the job?" "It's ______ me!"
3. I can't make heads or tails ______ of this report.
4. We're trying to come to grips ______ this new system.
5. Have you gotten a handle ______ the way this works yet?
6. I'm trying to get my head ______ these sales figures.
7. Most of what she says goes right ______ his head.

B *Missing verbs*

Complete these sentences by adding a verb. Use the correct tense.

1. The key seems to be knowing how to ___connect___ the dots.
2. We read the text again, but we ______ still none the wiser.
3. OK, so do you ______ my drift now?
4. It's OK. I ______ the picture now.
5. Business was better than ever. Then they closed the store – ______ figure!
6. Sorry, can you repeat that? I keep ______ the thread.
7. To be honest, I think Jo is ______ the point.
8. We saw them together a few times and just ______ two and two together.

Focus on use

A *Formality*

Rewrite this detective story to make it sound more natural. Replace the words in blue with idioms from the box.

be none the wiser	connect the dots	put two and two together
beyond me	get a fix on	

It was a difficult case. I'd been trying to understand (1) .... it for weeks. But I was not able to understand (2) ....

I looked at the pictures again and again. Some coal, a scarf, and a carrot lying on a lawn – why? It was impossible to understand (3) ....

Suddenly, I understood how everything was related (4) .... I used the information I had (5) .... Some kids made a snowman.

Then the weather got warm and the snow melted. Another successful case!

B *Over to you*

1. Do you know any techniques or strategies for understanding new and unfamiliar words or phrases in English? What are they?

2. Are there sayings or idioms that mean the same as ***lose the thread (of something)*** *or* ***something goes over your head*** *in your language? What are they?*

Now write

Write about a problem, situation, or puzzle that was difficult to understand at first. Did you understand it in the end? Use some idioms from the unit.

Unit 18
Work

(8:15 a.m.)

Sylvia: Lynne, the Chicago branch has farmed out an important account to us. We want you to handle it.

Lynne: Really?

Sylvia: Yes. You did a great job filling in for Martin while he was sick. Now you are going to have your work cut out for you, but I know you can do it.

Lynne: Thanks. I'll roll up my sleeves and get started right away.

(7:30 p.m.)

Marnie: Come on, Lynne. It's time to knock off for the day.

Jae: Yeah, we're going to the café across the street. Come with us – all work and no play . . .

Lynne: As long as you promise not to talk shop!

At work

- **on the job** while working
- **all in a day's work** unusual for other people to do but normal in your job
- **the bottom of the ladder** the lowest level or position
- **the top of the ladder** the highest level or position
- **fill in (for someone)** to do someone else's job temporarily
- **work hand in glove with someone / something** to work closely with someone or something
- **farm out** to give work or responsibilities to other people
- ⚠ **fall down on the job** to fail to do something at work
- **go over someone's head** to deal directly with someone at a higher level

Hard work

- **roll up your sleeves,** *also* **roll your sleeves up** to prepare for hard work
- **do the dirty work** to do the unpleasant or difficult things
- **get your hands dirty,** *also* **dirty your hands** to do work that is basic to something
- **have your work cut out for you** to have to do something that you know will be difficult

After work

- **all work and no play (makes Jack a dull boy)** it is not good to work all the time
- **knock off (for the day)** to stop working (for a period of time)
- **talk shop** to talk about the job when you are not working

Focus on meaning

Matching

Match the idioms with their definitions.

1. all in a day's work
2. all work and no play
3. do the dirty work
4. fall down on the job
5. farm out
6. fill in (for someone)
7. get your hands dirty
8. go over someone's head
9. have your work cut out for you
10. knock off (for the day)
11. on the job
12. roll up your sleeves
13. talk shop
14. the bottom of the ladder
15. the top of ladder
16. work hand in glove with someone

a. it is not good to work all the time
b. the highest level or position
c. the lowest rank
d. to deal with someone at a higher level
e. to do someone else's job temporarily
f. to do the unpleasant things
g. to fail to do something that you were expected to do
h. to give work to other people
i. to have a task that you know is difficult
j. to involve yourself in work that is basic to something
k. to prepare for hard work
l. to stop working for a time
m. to work closely with someone
n. to talk about work when you're not on the job
o. unusual for other people to do but not unusual for you
p. while working

Focus on form

A *Sentence completion*

Use these pairs of words to complete the sentences below.

all, day's	fill, for	over, head	work, out
bottom, ladder	hand, glove	roll, sleeves	work, play

1. Take some time off! All ___work___ and no ___play___ . . .
2. It's time to ________ up your ________ and get started.
3. This project isn't going to be easy. She really has her ________ cut ________ for her.
4. Thanks. It was nice of you to ________ in ________ me while I was sick.
5. They went ________ his ________ and contacted the managing director.
6. The school has been working ________ in ________ with the local police on this.
7. Meetings in three different cities on the same day – it's ________ in a ________ work for him.
8. This job may be at the ________ of the ________, but it's a very short ladder!

B *Correct or incorrect?*

Are these sentences correct? Some have an extra word. Put a check (✔) in the box if the sentence is correct. Put an ✘ in the box and circle the extra word if it is wrong.

1. I can't take credit for everything. Pete did a lot of the dirty work. ☑
2. We can't afford to fall down in on the job. ☐
3. I hope you're not afraid to get your hands on dirty. ☐
4. The sun's shining. Let's knock off early today. ☐
5. We're not permitted to use our cell phones on the job. ☐
6. Come on. This is a party. We shouldn't talk about shop. ☐
7. Let's farm out one of the projects and do the other one ourselves. ☐

Focus on use

A *Formality*

*Look at this e-mail from Elaine to her friend Glyn. It sounds very formal for an e-mail between friends. Replace the words in **bold** with phrases from the box to make the e-mail sound more friendly and natural. You will need to change the form of some words.*

all in a day's work	fill in	roll up your sleeves
fall down on the job	go over someone's head	

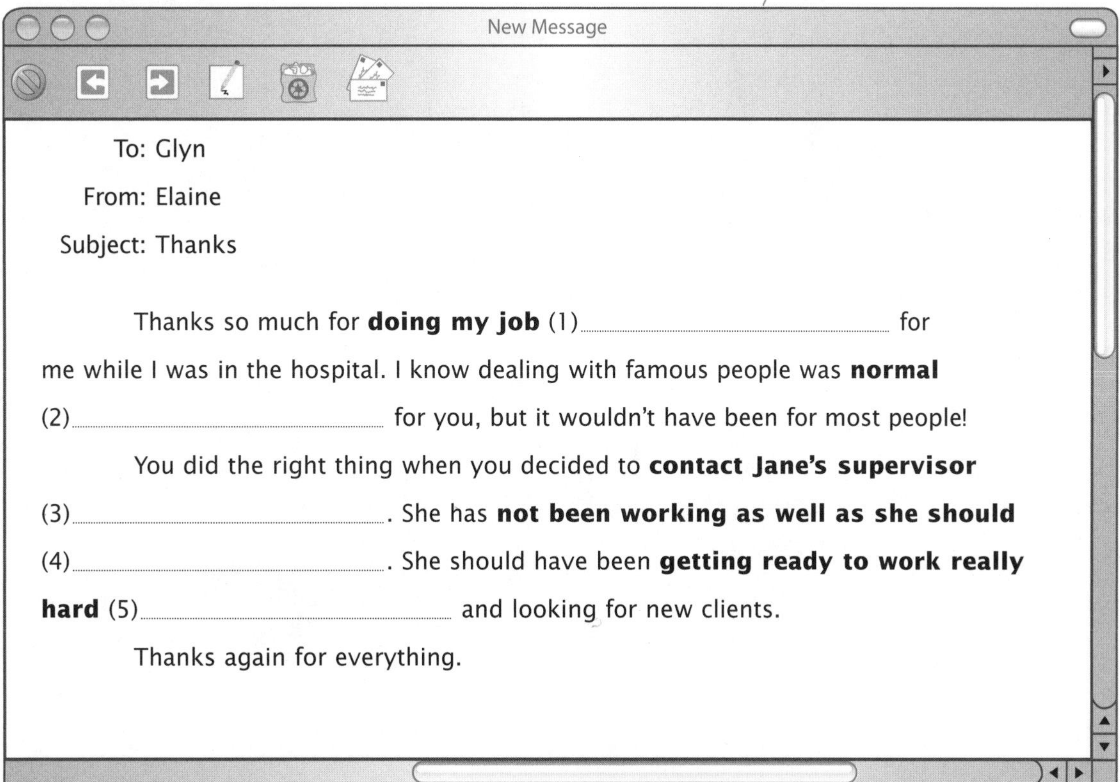

New Message

To: Glyn

From: Elaine

Subject: Thanks

Thanks so much for **doing my job** (1) .... for me while I was in the hospital. I know dealing with famous people was **normal** (2) .... for you, but it wouldn't have been for most people!

You did the right thing when you decided to **contact Jane's supervisor** (3) .... She has **not been working as well as she should** (4) .... She should have been **getting ready to work really hard** (5) .... and looking for new clients.

Thanks again for everything.

B *Over to you*

*In what situations do you think it is right to **go over someone's head**? Have you ever **gone over someone's head**? Was it the right thing to do?*

Now write

Think of a profession you are interested in. What would you need to do to get from **the bottom of the ladder** to the top? How long do you think it would take? What kind of personality would you need? Write a paragraph describing how you might climb from the bottom to **the top of the ladder**.

Unit 19

Ability

Ability to do something

- **a feel for something** an understanding or ability in a particular subject or activity
- **a mind of your own** the ability to act or think independently
- **a nose for something** a special ability to find or do something
- **the world is your oyster** you have the ability and the freedom to do exactly what you want

It's great traveling with Lou – she's got ***a nose for a good hotel****.*

Natural ability

- **born to do something** to have the natural ability to do something
- **have a head for something** to have a natural ability to do something well
- **have it in you** to possess a particular ability

Believing that someone has ability

- **credit someone with something** to believe that someone has a particular quality or ability
- **feel your oats** to have great confidence in your importance or ability
- **pride yourself on something** to value a special ability that you have

He ***prides himself on*** *his cooking.*

Demonstrating ability

- **fly by the seat of your pants** to do something difficult without the necessary experience or ability
- **in your own right,** *also* **in its own right** because of your own ability or effort
- **put someone through his / her paces** *also* **put something through its paces** to test the ability or skill of a person or a system
- **run rings around someone / something** to show much more skill or ability than someone or something else

Toni ***ran rings around*** *all the other players.*

Focus on meaning

Matching

Match the idioms with their short definitions. The key words in each definition are in blue.

1. the world is your oyster
2. a mind of your own
3. a nose for something
4. born to do something
5. credit someone with something
6. feel your oats
7. fly by the seat of your pants
8. have it in you
9. in your own right, *also* in its own right
10. pride yourself on something
11. put someone through his / her paces
12. run rings around someone / something
13. a feel for something
14. have a head for something

a. because of your own ability or effort
b. believe that someone has an ability
c. have confidence in your ability
d. do something without experience or ability
e. have the ability and freedom to do whatever you want
f. natural ability
g. an ability to do a task or to understand a subject
h. show more ability than someone else
i. possess a particular ability
j. to test ability
k. an ability to act or think independently
l. an ability to find or do something
m. have a natural ability to do something well
n. to value an ability you have

*You've finished school, and **the world is your oyster!***

Focus on form

A *Sentence completion*

Use these pairs of words to complete the sentences below.

born, to	got, feel	mind, own	seat, pants
feeling, oats	has, nose	run, rings	world, oyster

1. I studied piano for a year, but I never really ....got.... a ....feel.... for it.
2. I advised her to accept the job offer, but she has a .... of her ...., so I don't know what she'll decide.
3. Any good journalist .... a .... for a good story.
4. Workers are .... their .... and demanding higher wages.
5. None of us had ever worked on a magazine before, so we were flying by the .... of our ....
6. This sweet-voiced artist was .... sing.
7. International gangs of art thieves have .... around the national police.
8. The .... is your .... when you're young, healthy, and free to go anywhere.

B *Prepositions*

Use some, but not all, of the prepositions in the box to complete the sentences. You may need to use a preposition twice.

above	for	in	of	on	through	to	under	with

1. He prides himself ....on.... his teaching.
2. I never had a head .... music.
3. I credited her .... more sense than she showed.
4. This contest will put you .... your paces.
5. His speech was really funny – we didn't know he had it .... him.
6. His whole family were writers, but he became even more famous .... his own right.

Focus on use

A *Formality*

Make this interview sound more natural. Replace the phrases in blue with idioms from the unit.

Interviewer: So you won! Island Survival certainly tested your survival ability (1) ...., didn't it? Did you have survival training before you went?

Survivor 1: Not really. Most of the time we were just doing it for the first time (2) ....!

Interviewer: How do you feel?

Survivor 2: Amazing! I didn't think we would be able to do it (3) ....!

Interviewer: You actually did much better than (4) .... the others. Why do you think that was?

Survivor 1: Well, we were lucky because Fred here has a natural ability for (5) .... solving puzzles.

Survivor 2: And you are really good at finding (6) .... fresh water and food!

B *Over to you*

The idiom ***the world is your oyster*** *comes from Shakespeare's play* The Merry Wives of Windsor. *Oysters are expensive now, but they were a very common food in Shakespeare's England. What idiom or saying in your language means the same as* ***the world is your oyster****?*

Now write

Write about someone you know who **has a mind of his** or **her own**. Give an example of how this person does things independently.

Unit 20 Age

Sally: Jim! Great to see you again after all these years! You haven't changed a bit! You look great!

Jim: Thanks, Sally. Well, we're all of a certain age, aren't we?

Sally: Is that Miss Livesay, the English teacher? She's getting on in years, isn't she? I thought they put her out to pasture years ago.

Jim: She was well past her prime when she taught us. Look, there's Mr. McCoy, the art teacher. I guess he's over the hill, too.

Sally: I think this was the first high school he taught at. He was still wet behind the ears when he started here.

Jim: Yes, but he's looking a bit long in the tooth now, isn't he?

Sally: Do you hear that song? Wow! That's a blast from the past.

Jim: It sure is. And the sound system is on its last legs. I think it's the same one they had when we were here.

Describing people

- **getting on in years** becoming old
- ⚠ **of a certain age** middle-aged or older; not young
- ⚠ **long in the tooth** very old
- ⚠ **over the hill**, *also* **past your / its prime** no longer able to do things as well as before because of age
- **put (someone) out to pasture** make someone stop working
- ⚠ **wet behind the ears** young and without much experience
- ⚠ **live in the past** to have old-fashioned ideas
- ⚠ **behind the times** old-fashioned

Describing things, ideas, and sometimes people

- **have seen better days** to be no longer in good condition
- **on its last legs** about to stop working
- **a blast from the past** something that brings back memories of old times
- **as old as the hills** extremely old

Focus on meaning

A *Matching*

Match the idioms on the right with their definitions on the left.

1. people who are old or getting older (indirect)
2. people who are older (direct)
3. people who do not do things as well as they used to
4. old-fashioned
5. something that reminds you of earlier times
6. constantly thinking about people or events from the past
7. someone who is young and inexperienced
8. very, very old

a. long in the tooth, over the hill
b. getting on in years, of a certain age
c. past your prime
d. a blast from the past
e. behind the times
f. wet behind the ears
g. as old as the hills
h. living in the past

B *Sentence completion*

Use idioms from the unit to complete the following sentences.

1. Our car is getting older; it has seen better days.
2. This is her first job. She's still ....
3. Face it. Things have changed. You can't .... anymore.
4. We may be ...., but we're too young to be ....
5. My father is seriously .... when it comes to fashion.
6. It was the classic boy meets girl plot – as ....
7. This DVD player is wearing out. It's ....
8. My father-in-law is .... in ...., but he still plays golf twice a week.

Focus on form

A *Prepositions*

Use the prepositions in the box to complete the sentences. You will need to use some of the prepositions more than once.

behind	from	in	on	out	past	to

1. Businesses can't be ..behind.. the times when it comes to technology.
2. Several of his colleagues were put .... pasture.
3. Hula hoops! Now those really are a blast .... the past.
4. Actresses over fifty are not .... their prime.
5. This computer is .... its last legs.
6. There is no such thing as a "job for life" anymore. You're living .... the past.
7. He's a bit long .... the tooth to be out clubbing, isn't he?
8. This is his first job. He's still a bit wet .... the ears.

B *Correct or incorrect?*

Are these sentences correct? Some have an extra word. Put a check (✔) in the box if the sentence is correct. Put an ✘ in the box and circle the extra word if it is wrong.

1. At forty, you are not (out) over the hill. ☒
2. We're all getting on in years. ☐
3. He's a bit long in the tooth to be playing a nineteen year old, isn't he? ☐
4. That song is a real blast from out the past! ☐
5. It's a story that's as old as is the hills. ☐
6. This old coat has seen to better days. ☐
7. I was wet from behind the ears when I started my first job. ☐

Focus on use

A *Formality*

Use the idioms in the box to replace the phrases in blue in the dialog.

a blast from the past	on its last legs	put you out to pasture
getting on in years	past your prime	seen better days

Anna: How do you like your new digital camera?

Steve: It's great, but I need a new computer to go with it. My old one is about to stop working (1)..

Anna: I see what you mean. It was fantastic when you bought it, but it's not as good as it used to be (2)..

Steve: Yeah, it's a bit like me. I'm also not as good as I used to be (3)..

Anna: Oh come on. You may be becoming older (4).., but it's not time to make you stop working (5)..

Steve: Have a look at this old box camera over here.

Anna: Now that is something that brings back memories (6)..!

B *Over to you*

1. *Have you ever felt that you were* ***wet behind the ears*** *in a new situation? Describe what happened.*
2. *Do you know anyone who is sensitive about his or her age – either old or young? Explain.*

Now write

Write a short description of a person or a thing that is old or getting older. Use some of the idioms from this unit in your description.

Unit 21 Criticism

Criticizing someone or something

- **beat someone up,** *also* **beat up someone** to criticize someone strongly
- **bite the hand that feeds you** to severely criticize the person or organization that helps you or pays you
- **cast aspersions on someone / something** to say that someone's character or work is bad
- **open season (on something / someone)** a situation in which someone or something is criticized

She feels as if someone has declared ***open season on lawyers.***

- **give someone a hard time** to criticize or make life difficult for someone
- **go after someone / something** to attack or try to hurt someone or something
- **jump all over someone** to criticize someone severely
- **knock something down** to show that an idea or an opinion is completely wrong
- **look a gift horse in the mouth** to criticize or refuse to accept something that has been offered to you
- **make fun of someone / something,** *also* **poke fun at someone / something** to make someone or something seem foolish by making jokes about the person or thing
- **tear someone / something apart** to severely criticize someone or something

His teachers ***tore him apart*** *for cheating on the test.*

Being criticized

- **on the firing line** in a situation that attracts criticism
- **in the line of fire** in a situation in which you may be severely criticized
- **draw fire** to attract criticism
- **under fire** being criticized for something you have done

Focus on meaning

Concept map

Complete this concept map, using the idioms in the box.

a. under fire
b. open season on something / someone
c. beat someone up
d. bite the hand that feeds you
e. cast aspersions on someone / something
f. draw fire
g. give someone a hard time
h. go after someone / something
i. in the line of fire
j. jump all over someone
k. knock something down
l. look a gift horse in the mouth
m. make fun of someone / something
n. on the firing line
o. tear someone / something apart

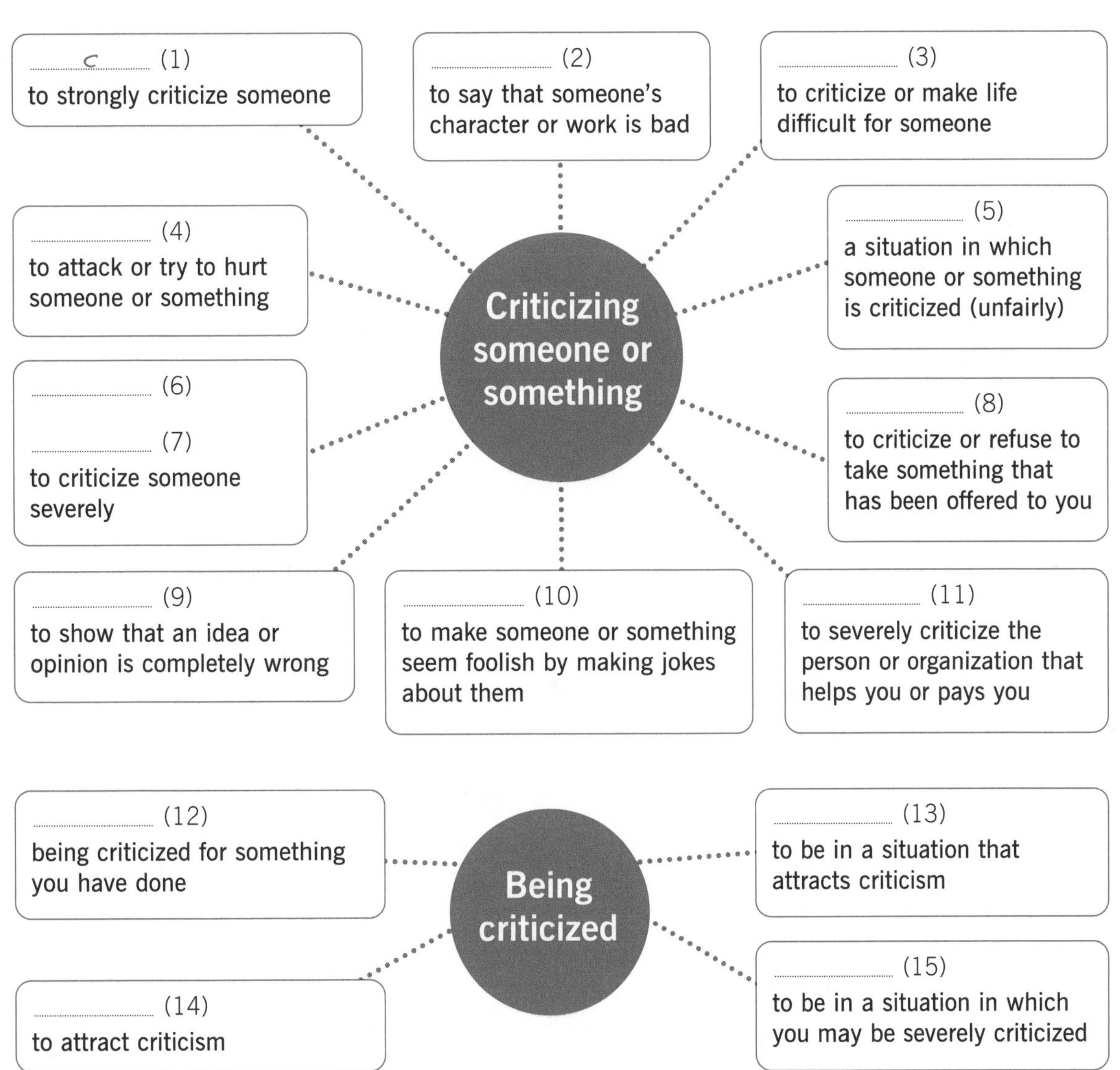

Focus on form

A *Beginnings and endings*

Match the beginnings and endings of these idioms.

Beginnings	Endings
1. bite the hand	a. apart
2. open	b. fire
3. draw	c. hard time
4. give someone a	d. in the mouth
5. in the firing	e. of fire
6. in the line	f. line
7. look a gift horse	g. of someone
8. make fun	h. season on something / someone
9. tear someone	i. that feeds you

B *Preposition crossword*

Complete the crossword by filling in the missing preposition in each idiom.

Across

1 (come) ...... fire (5)

3 cast aspersions ...... (2)

4 go ...... someone (5)

Down

1 beat someone ...... (2)

2 knock something ...... (4)

3 jump all ...... someone (4)

Focus on use

A *What do you say?*

Use the idioms from the unit to complete the responses to these statements.

1. "I said the company was ripping off their customers, and they fired me!"

   "That's what you get for ____________________."

2. "Granddad gave me a DVD player, but I'd rather have a newer model."

   "Don't ____________________."

3. "He walks like a duck."

   "Stop that! You shouldn't ____________________."

4. "You know, this is not going to be a popular decision."

   "You're right. It's probably going to ____________________."

5. "I admire her. She isn't afraid to take responsibility when things go wrong."

   "No, she's willing to put herself ____________________."

6. "I don't understand why the reviewers have all been so negative about the film."

   "I know. It's like they all decided to ____________________."

B *Over to you*

1. *The idiom "to look a gift horse in the mouth" comes from the fact that a horse's age can be estimated by checking how worn its teeth are. So, looking a gift horse in the mouth was seen as a criticism of the gift. Is there a similar idiom in your language? What is it?*
2. *Think of idioms in your language that mean "to criticize" or "to be criticized." Is the main metaphor (hurting, injuring, or destroying) the same as it is in English? If not, what is it?*

Now write

Write a paragraph about a time in your life when you either criticized someone or were criticized by someone. Use idioms from the unit.

Unit 22

Danger

Doing something dangerous

- **play Russian roulette** to take foolish and dangerous risks
- **put your life on the line** to risk dying
- **risk your neck** to do something dangerous
- **stick your neck out,** *also* **stick out your neck** to take a risk

*We **risked our necks** to rescue you, and all you can say is "Thanks"?*

Trying to avoid danger

- **hit the deck,** *or* **hit the dirt** to fall to the ground suddenly to avoid danger
- **on your guard** to be careful and aware because a situation might be dangerous
- **walk a tightrope** to act carefully to avoid a dangerous situation
- **watch your step** to be careful in a situation that could be dangerous

*Mom's practicing again – **hit the deck**!*

In a dangerous situation

- **in jeopardy** in danger
- **lay someone / something open to something** to put someone or something in danger
- **when the chips are down** when you are in a difficult or dangerous situation

*Fiona's injury put her basketball career **in jeopardy**.*

Describing danger

- **on the loose** free to move about and dangerous
- **too hot to handle** too dangerous or difficult to deal with
- **blow the whistle (on someone / something)** to show dangerous conditions or illegal activities

*I knew my company was polluting the water, so I **blew the whistle** on them.*

Focus on meaning

A *Grouping*

Put the idioms in the box into the correct group.

a. blow the whistle
b. hit the deck
c. in jeopardy
d. lay something open to something
e. on the loose
f. on your guard
g. play Russian roulette
h. put your life on the line
i. risk your neck
j. stick your neck out, *also* stick out your neck
k. too hot to handle
l. walk a tightrope
m. watch your step
n. when the chips are down

1 To do something dangerous

g. play Russian roulette
____
____
____

2 Dangerous

a. blow the whistle
____
____

3 In a dangerous situation

c. in jeopardy
____
____

4 Trying to avoid danger

b. hit the deck
____
____
____

B *Sentence completion*

Use idioms from the box in Exercise A to complete the following sentences. You may have to change the form of some words.

1. Two of the escaped prisoners are still on the loose.
2. You have to be brave to __________ on a big company like that.
3. Most people are not willing to __________ their __________ for a cause.
4. She's friendly when you get to know her, but she's always __________ around strangers.

Focus on form

A *Danger crossword*

Complete the crossword by filling in the missing word in each idiom.

Across

1 .... a tightrope (4)

4 .... Russian roulette (4)

5 in .... (8)

7 blow the .... (7)

10 risk your .... (4)

Down

2 put your life on the .... (4)

3 too hot to .... (6)

6 lay something .... to something (4)

7 .... your step (5)

8 .... your neck out (5)

9 on the .... (5)

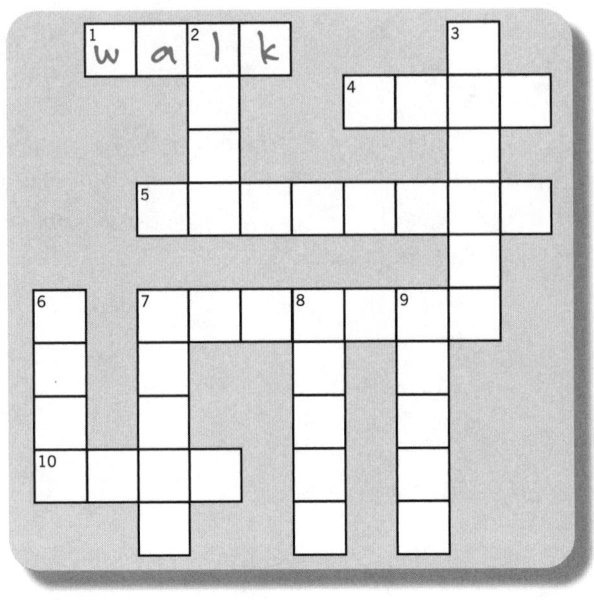

B *Scrambled sentences*

Put the words in these sentences into the correct order.

1. hit – Quick deck the!

   Quick - hit the deck!

2. all need the You guard be to on time your.

   ....

3. kid The hit a snowball, so I the threw dirt.

   ....

4. great She's a when the friend are down chips.

   ....

Focus on use

A *Describing danger*

Rewrite the phrases in blue in this football commentary to make it sound more natural and exciting.

The Lambs have been acting carefully to avoid danger (1) .... today, but it looks like Jones is going to change all that and finally do something dangerous (2) ....

The Pandas are suddenly careful and aware (3) .... They know that their win could be in danger (4) .... and they have got to be careful (5) .... !

But there goes Jones! He's free to move around (6) .... now! Touchdown! He's done it! The crowd is going crazy! Jones is the man you want on your team when you are in a dangerous situation (7) .... !

B *Over to you*

In which of these situations do you feel that a person should ***blow the whistle****? Why?*

1. *A coworker is using company time to build a Web site for his new business.*
2. *A coworker is making photocopies on the office machine for a charity event.*
3. *A student who has no money is living in the college library.*
4. *Some students are copying their essays off the Internet.*

Now write

Write about a person you know or have heard about who has put his or her **life on the line**. Describe the person, the situation, and the reason for the action he or she took.

Unit 23

Search and discover

Dear Rachel,

Good news! I think we have **stumbled across** the perfect house! We were reading the papers and searching the Internet – really **beating the bushes** – but we weren't having any luck **tracking down** our dream home in the country.

Then it **dawned on us** – we needed to spend a few weekends **nosing around** some of the little towns near the state park.

You'll love the place, too. . .

Searching

- **beat the bushes** to search everywhere for someone or something
- **leave no stone unturned** to do everything possible to achieve or find something
- **a needle in a haystack** something extremely hard to find
- **nose around** to try to discover information
- ⚠ **poke your nose into something,** *also* **stick your nose into something** to try to discover things that do not involve you
- **throw someone off the scent** to give someone false or confusing information so that the person will not discover something

Discovering

- **come to light** to become known
- **dawn on you** to suddenly understand something
- **ferret out something,** *also* **ferret something out** to discover something after careful searching
- **read between the lines** to find a hidden meaning in something said or written
- **reinvent the wheel** to take time and effort to do something that has already been done
- **sniff out someone / something,** *also* **sniff someone /something out** to discover someone or something, usually only after a special effort
- **stumble across someone / something,** *also* **stumble on someone / something** to meet someone or find something unexpectedly
- **track down someone / something,** *also* **track someone / something down** to find someone or something after searching for the person or thing

Focus on meaning

Correct or incorrect?

Below each numbered sentence is a restatement of it. Put a check (✔) in the box if the restatement is correct. If it is incorrect, put an ✘ in the box and correct it.

1. Trying to find anything in his office is like looking for a needle in a haystack.
   It's extremely dangerous to look for anything in his office.
   ☒ It's extremely difficult to find anything in his office.
2. They finally tracked him down in a hotel downtown.
   They unexpectedly found him in a hotel downtown.
   ☐ ....
3. She stumbled across an old letter of his.
   She had been looking for an old letter of his.
   ☐ ....
4. Their job is to sniff out talented new singers
   Their job is to decide which new singers are talented.
   ☐ ....
5. The police were thrown off the scent by two of the witnesses.
   The police were helped by two of the witnesses.
   ☐ ....
6. The story came to light last summer.
   The story became known last summer.
   ☐ ....
7. You're reinventing the wheel.
   You're doing something that has already been done before.
   ☐ ....
8. There was a reporter nosing around the office today.
   There was a reporter looking for information at the office today.
   ☐ ....
9. We will leave no stone unturned.
   We are going to do everything we can to find it.
   ☐ ....
10. It dawned on me that I didn't need to call him back.
    I realized that I didn't need to call him back.
    ☐ ....
11. We've beaten the bushes but haven't found anything.
    We've looked everywhere, but we haven't found anything.
    ☐ ....

Focus on form

A *Prepositions and adverbs*

Use some, but not all, of the prepositions and adverbs in the box to complete the sentences. You will need to use some of them more than once.

between	down	in	into	on	out	over	to

1. I'm trying to track ___down___ one of my old classmates from college.
2. Police officers stumbled ______ the drugs when they were on a routine patrol.
3. The FBI knew they had a double agent in their midst, but it took years to sniff him ______.
4. The report doesn't criticize the research directly, but you can read ______ the lines that the review committee wasn't impressed.
5. Officials say they will ferret ______ abuses in the welfare program.
6. Four soldiers have faced charges since the scandal came ______ light last fall.
7. It's pretty much a needle ______ a haystack because these are extremely hard to find.
8. The government has no business poking its nose ______ people's personal lives.

B *Beginnings and endings*

Match the beginnings and endings of these sentences.

1. It suddenly dawned
2. They were nosing
3. There's no point in reinventing
4. We will leave no
5. We tried to throw
6. They've been beating

a. stone unturned in our search for the truth.
b. them off the scent.
c. around here this morning.
d. the wheel.
e. the bushes around here.
f. on him that she'd been joking.

Focus on use

A *Sentence completion*

Use idioms from the unit to complete this posting on a message board.

Message Board

#36 Hi,

Posted: 3:36 p.m.

I wonder if anyone out there can help me.

I'm really glad I (1) ______________ this site!

I'm trying to (2) ______________ my old college roommate. It's a bit like trying to find a (3) ______________, because she has a really common name – Mary Smith. I've been looking everywhere for her. I've really been (4) ______________ but haven't found her yet.

Here are her details . . .

Post Quote Reply

B *Over to you*

Are there idioms in your language that mean the same as a ***needle in a haystack*** *and* ***reinvent the wheel****? What are they?*

Now write

Choose one of the statements below and write a paragraph agreeing or disagreeing with the statement.

1. Governments have no right to **poke their noses** into people's private lives.
2. There are no more discoveries to be made. Most research is just **reinventing the wheel**.
3. The Internet has made it too easy to **track people down**.

Unit 24

Easy/difficult

Andy: Now don't worry. Learning to use this new software is as easy as pie. It's a piece of cake.

Ray: I'm not so sure. The manual was as clear as mud.

Andy: I'll show it to you step by step. Once you've seen it, you could run it with one hand tied behind your back.

Easy

- **(as) easy as pie** very easy
- **a piece of cake** something very easy
- **like taking candy from a baby** extremely easy
- **(as) plain as day** easy to see or understand
- **it doesn't take a rocket scientist to do something** it is easy to understand something
- **do something with your eyes closed** to do something very easily
- **do something with one hand / arm tied behind your back** to do something very easily
- **the path of least resistance** the way that is the easiest

*She decided to take **the path of least resistance**.*

Difficult

- ⚠ **(as) clear as mud** very difficult to understand
- ⚠ **hell on wheels** extremely difficult
- ⚠ **like pulling teeth** extremely difficult
- **something is not a bed of roses** something is not easy and without trouble.
- **a tough row to hoe** a difficult situation to deal with
- **through the wringer** experiencing something very difficult or unpleasant
- **turn the corner** improve after going through something very difficult

*Things have been bad, but I think I'm about to **turn the corner**.*

Focus on meaning

Concept map

Complete this concept map, using the idioms in the box.

a. (as) easy as pie
b. a piece of cake
c. a tough row to hoe
d. (as) clear as mud
e. (as) plain as day
f. do something with your eyes closed
g. do something with one hand/arm tied behind your back
h. hell on wheels
i. it doesn't take a rocket scientist to do something
j. like pulling teeth
k. like taking candy from a baby
l. something is not a bed of roses
m. the path of least resistance
n. through the wringer
o. turn the corner

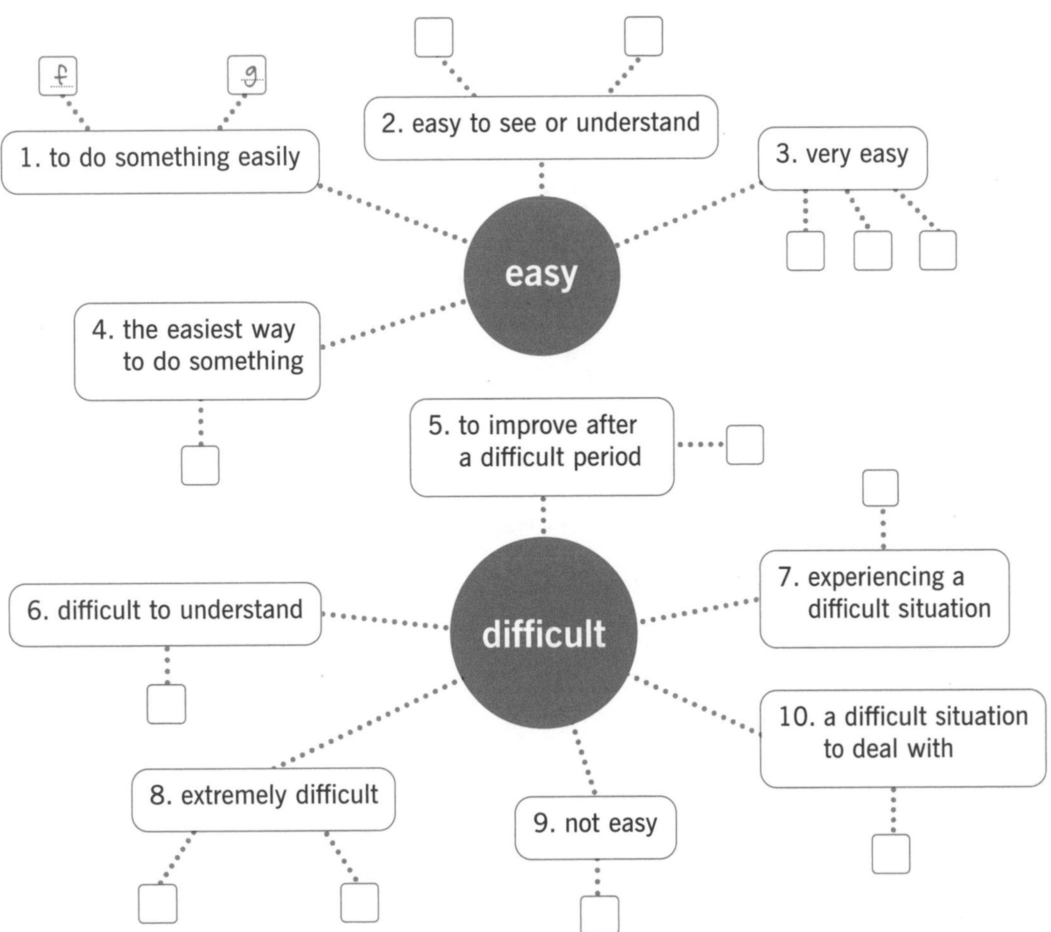

Focus on form

Sentence completion

Use the words from the box to fill in the missing words in each idiom.

behind	corner	mud	pulling	roses
cake	easy	path	rocket	through
candy	eyes	plain	row	wheels

1. You make it sound as ____easy____ as pie.
2. This exam is going to be a piece of ________.
3. Graduate students have a tough ________ to hoe.
4. His directions were as clear as ________.
5. I looked at the list of winners, and there was my name, ________ as day.
6. I've filled this form in so many times I could do it with my ________ closed.
7. Taking good pictures is so simple you could do it with one hand tied ________ your back.
8. He's going to be hell on ________ to deal with.
9. It doesn't take a ________ scientist to see that this program doesn't work.
10. Getting our kids dressed and off to school is like ________ teeth.
11. Selling these cars is like taking ________ from a baby – people love them.
12. He discovered that living in a foreign country is not always a bed of ________.
13. Thieves usually take the ________ of least resistance and steal cars that aren't locked.
14. Mr. Gold went ________ the wringer to get immigration papers for his parents.
15. I wonder if the country has really turned the ________ in this crisis.

Focus on use

A *Sentence completion*

Complete this dialog using either "easy" or "difficult" idioms from the unit.

Have I ever told you about the time I tried to teach Einstein to drive? You might think it would have been like .... (1 – easy). After all, he was really smart. But it was more like .... (2 – difficult)! It was really a .... (3 – difficult)!

I said, "OK, Albert. Now there is nothing to worry about – this is going to be as .... (4 – easy), a .... (5 – easy)! You could do this .... (6 – easy) or .... (7 – easy)! But that wouldn't be a very good idea would it? Ha ha."

Teaching Einstein to drive.

He didn't laugh. He just looked at me and said, "Explain what you want me to do again, will you? It was .... (8 – difficult to understand) the first time."

I said, "Of course," but I thought I'd made it .... (9 – easy to understand). Oh, he really put me .... (10 – difficult)!

In fact, that was when I decided to quit teaching driving and become a rocket scientist.

B *Over to you*

Where do idioms come from? The idiom ***a tough row to hoe*** *comes from farming: seeds are planted in rows (lines) and are kept free of weeds (unwanted wild plants) using a hoe (a garden tool).*

Think about idioms for "easy" and "difficult" in your own language. Where do they come from? Which ones are similar to English idioms?

Now write

Describe something you have done that was difficult to begin with but became easier at some point. Use idioms from the unit.

Unit 25

Failure

- **go belly up,** *also* **hit the skids** *or* **strike out** to fail
- ⚠ **fall flat (on your face)** to fail completely
- ⚠ **crash and burn** to fail suddenly and completely
- **blow up in your face,** *also* **explode in your face** to fail unexpectedly
- **come apart at the seams** to be in a bad condition and about to fail or lose control

We've seen several restaurants ***go belly up*** *in this town.*

It used to be a really good school, but it's slowly ***coming apart at the seams.***

- ⚠ **drop the ball** to fail to keep working to reach a goal
- **(go) back to drawing board** to start something again because the last attempt failed
- **psych someone out,** *also* **psych out someone** to make a person believe that he or she will fail
- **throw a monkey wrench into something** to cause something to fail

- **throw in the towel** to admit defeat or failure
- **something will never fly** something will not succeed
- **go down the tubes** [especially spoken] to fail or become much worse
- ⚠ **wash out (of something)** to leave a program or activity because you failed to meet its standards

This is the fourth time she's taken the test, and she's completely ***psyched herself out.***

Focus on meaning

Sentence transformation

Rewrite these sentences, using the words in parentheses.

1. It was my first presentation, and I was worried that I would fail completely. (fall / face)

   It was my first presentation, and I was worried that I would fall flat on my face.

2. It's just not good enough – we'll have to do it again. (drawing board)

3. She watched her parents' marriage suddenly fail. (crash / burn)

4. We try to make the other team believe that they will lose before the game begins. (psych)

5. People told him it was a great story but it would not succeed as a movie. (fly)

6. In the past, our ads have been successful, but this time we failed. (strike)

7. The union had to admit defeat and settle its dispute with the company. (towel)

8. Public schools have stopped trying on arts education. (ball)

9. We keep trying to get together, but her crazy schedule keeps wrecking our plans. (monkeywrench)

10. His business is failing, and he's about to lose his house. (tubes)

11. His career really failed after his divorce. (skids)

12. All their plans suddenly failed unexpectedly. (blow up)

Focus on form

A *Beginnings and endings*

Match the beginnings and endings of these idioms.

1. blow up	a. the ball
2. come apart	b. someone out
3. drop	c. on your face
4. go back	d. in your face
5. crash and	e. out
6. fall flat	f. at the seams
7. throw a monkey wrench	g. the skids
8. throw in the	h. to the drawing board
9. go down	i. burn
10. hit	j. out
11. something will never	k. into something
12. strike	l. up
13. psych	m. towel
14. go belly	n. fly
15. wash	o. the tubes

B *Correct or incorrect?*

Are these sentences correct? Some have an extra word. Put a check (✓) in the box if the sentence is correct. Put an ✗ in the box and circle the extra word if it is wrong.

1. He's worried because the company is going down (to) the tubes. ☒
2. Make sure you don't drop the ball. ☐
3. They washed out of college and built their first computer in the garage. ☐
4. Well, it's back over to the drawing board. ☐
5. It's time to throw in on the towel. ☐

Focus on use

A *What do you say?*

Using idioms from the unit, what could you say in these situations?

1. A coworker says, "The customer didn't like the new design."

2. A good friend of yours who has a new job says, "The boss is expecting a lot from me."

3. Just before an important tennis match, a friend says, "She looks me right in the eye and seems so confident. I'll never beat her."

4. A friend at work says, "The marketing manager hated my ideas."

5. You agree with a fellow student who says, "I think the dean is losing control. What do you think?"

B *Over to you*

*Muhammad Ali used to **psych out** his opponents by predicting when in the fight he would knock them out. What are other ways that sports people **psych out** their opponents?*

Now write

Write a paragraph about either a project you were working on when someone **threw a monkey wrench** into it or a time when you had to go **back to the drawing board**.

Unit 26
Good and bad

Good

- **(the) top of the line** the very best of something
- **the greatest thing since sliced bread** *also* **the best thing since sliced bread** wonderful
- **worth its weight in gold** extremely useful or valuable
- **the cream of the crop** the best of a particular group
- **a tough act to follow,** *also* **a hard act to follow** so good that whatever happens next is not likely to seem as good
- **head and shoulders above someone / something** much better than similar people or things
- **make your mouth water** to feel pleasure at the thought of something particularly beautiful or good
- **the best of both worlds** the most enjoyable or attractive features of two different things
- **to die for** [especially spoken] extremely good
- **up to scratch** at an acceptable standard or quality

He's ***head and shoulders*** *above the rest of the team.*

Becoming bad

- **from the sublime to the ridiculous** from something that is very good to something that is very bad or silly
- **go from bad to worse** to become even more difficult or unpleasant

The neighborhood quickly ***goes from bad to worse.***

Bad

- **not all it's cracked up to be** not as good or as special as people believe
- **nothing to write home about** not something that is especially good or exciting
- ⚠ **the bottom of the barrel** the worst or the least able members of a group
- **the bottom of the heap,** *also* **the bottom of the pile** the lowest rank within a group

I always feel like I'm at ***the bottom of the heap*** *in the office.*

Focus on meaning

A *Matching*

Write the idiom under the picture that best describes it. If the idiom is positive, circle +; if the idiom is negative, circle –.

a tough act to follow	nothing to write home about
make your mouth water	the greatest thing since sliced bread
the bottom of the barrel	worth its weight in gold

1 
+ –

the bottom of the barrel

2 
+ –

....

3 
+ –

....

4 
+ –

....

5 

+ –

....

6 

+ –

....

B *Correct or incorrect?*

Below each numbered sentence is a restatement of it. Put a check (✔) in the box if the restatement is correct. If it is incorrect, put an ✘ in the box and correct it.

1. He's head and shoulders above the others. ☒ He's better than the others.
   He is taller than the others.
2. Business has gone from bad to worse. ☐ ....
   Business is not as good now as it was.
3. That course is not all it's cracked up to be. ☐ ....
   That course is not as good as people say it is.
4. The food was nothing to write home about. ☐ ....
   The food was not very special.
5. The chocolate cake is to die for. ☐ ....
   The chocolate cake will kill you.

Focus on form

A *Prepositions*

Use some, but not all, of the prepositions in the box to complete the sentences. You will need to use some of the prepositions more than once.

about	above	by	from	of	out	through	to	up

1. This staff isn't the cream ___of___ the crop, but it's not as bad as you say.
2. Chicago's baseball team may be the oldest, but it is still head and shoulders ______ the rest of the league.
3. I have the best ______ both worlds, because I live in the country but I'm only an hour from the city.
4. The four acts for the opening of the jazz festival were all top ______ the line.
5. The performances at the festival ranged from the sublime ______ the ridiculous.
6. We're giving him a week to bring the team ______ ______ scratch.
7. The Tigers lost their first game 25 to 0, and then things went ______ bad ______ worse.
8. The general opinion is that love affairs aren't all they're cracked ______ to be.
9. The food was all right but nothing to write home ______.

B *Beginnings and endings*

Match the beginnings and endings of these sentences.

Beginnings

1. The last mayor was one of the most beloved in the city's history –
2. We had apple pie, and
3. There were only 40 new students;
4. One look at the menu
5. User-friendly software is
6. Jay thinks his new car
7. Being near the bottom of the heap,

Endings

a. I think the admissions office was getting to the bottom of the barrel.
b. the company has nowhere to go but up.
c. is the greatest thing since sliced bread.
d. it was to die for.
e. was enough to make anyone's mouth water.
f. worth its weight in gold.
g. he was a tough act to follow.

Focus on use

A *Describing good and bad*

Using idioms from the unit, write a sentence about each of the following.

1. A performer (an actor, a musician) you think is very capable or talented

   ....

2. Some food that is *very* good

   ....

3. Something (a film, a play, or a concert) that was wasn't very good or interesting and became even less so

   ....

4. A place you went to that wasn't as much fun or as interesting as you expected it to be

   ....

5. A very useful Web site

   ....

6. A gadget or piece of technology that is the best of its kind

   ....

B *Over to you*

Can you think of an idiom in your language that means that something is very good and useful, like ***the greatest thing since sliced bread*** *or* ***worth its weight in gold****? Explain.*

Now write

Describe a situation that would be **the best of both worlds** for you.

Unit 27 Honesty

Truth

- **call a spade a spade** to tell the unpleasant truth about something
- **come clean** to tell the truth about something you have tried to hide
- **get to the bottom of something** to discover the truth about something
- **set the record straight** to tell the truth about something that has not been accurately reported
- **take something with a grain of salt** to consider something not to be completely true or right

I'll ***come clean*** *– I really don't know how to cook at all.*

Honesty

- **fair and square** honestly
- **lay it on the line** to be completely honest
- **make no bones about something** to say clearly what you think or feel about something
- **pull no punches** to deal with something honestly, without hiding anything
- **pull your / its punches** to deal with something in a way that is not completely honest or direct
- **on the level** honest or true
- **on the up and up** honest or legal

He ***made no bones about*** *how bad he thought the food was.*

Sincerity

- **from the bottom of your heart** [especially spoken] with sincere feeling
- **ring true** to seem accurate or sincere
- ⚠ **ring hollow,** *also* **ring false** to seem dishonest, not true, not sincere, or wrong

You have been so kind – we thank you ***from the bottom of our hearts****.*

Focus on meaning

Concept map

Complete this concept map, using the idioms in the box.

a. call a spade a spade
b. come clean
c. fair and square
d. from the bottom of your heart
e. get to the bottom of something
f. lay it on the line
g. make no bones about something
h. pull no punches
i. pull your punches
j. on the level
k. on the up and up
l. ring hollow
m. ring true
n. set the record straight
o. take something with a grain of salt

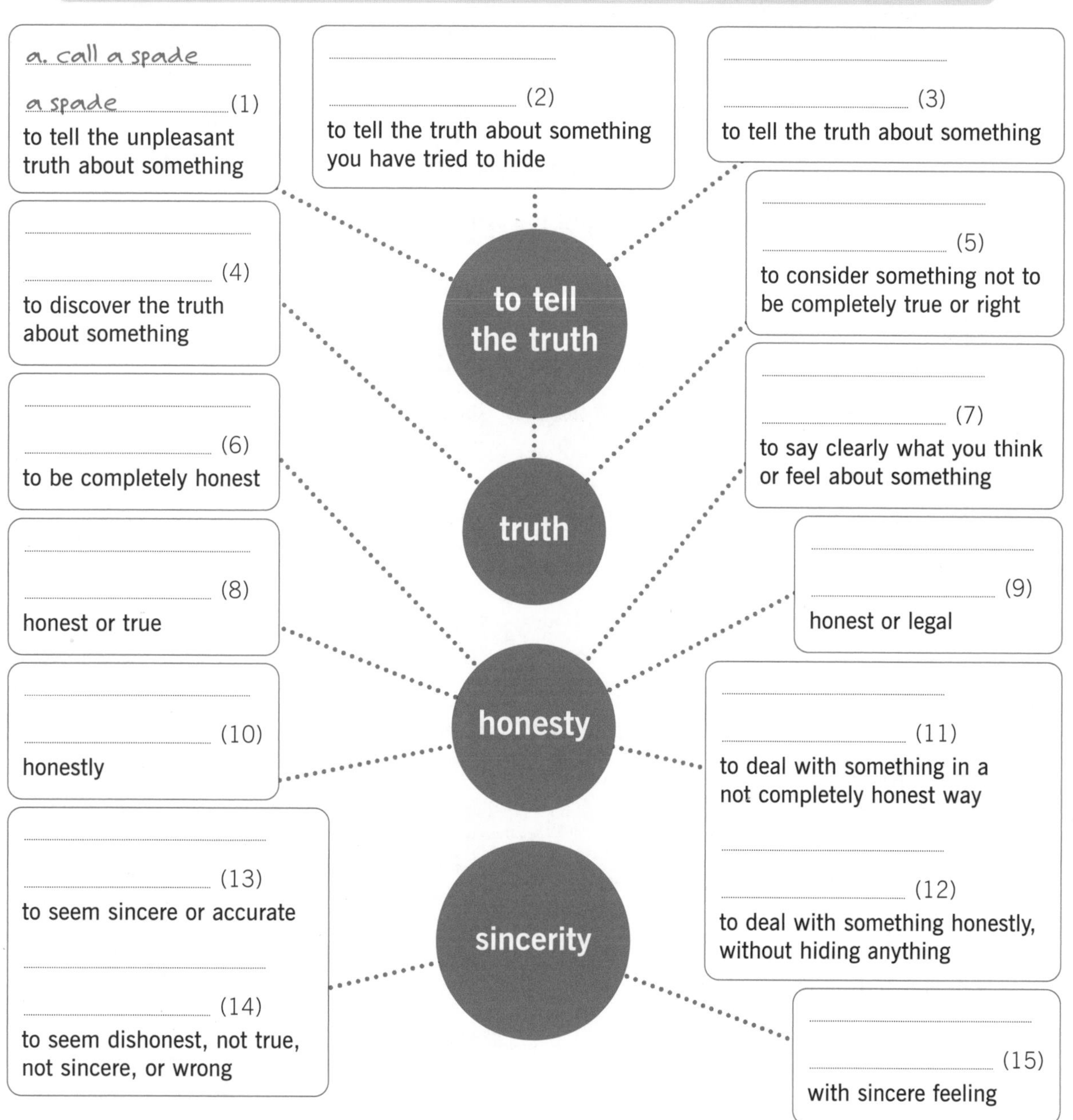

Focus on form

A *Detective story*

Use idioms from the unit to fill in the missing words in this detective story.

There was something about the Miller case that just didn't ring (1) ___true___. In my business you get used to taking what people say with a grain of (2) ______. But this time someone was lying.

I was sure Mrs. Miller was on the (3) ______, but I was not so sure about her husband. I decided to get to the (4) ______ of it. I would call Mr. Miller. I wouldn't (5) ______ any punches.

"Hello, Miller, this is Detective Flynn. I'm going to (6) ______ a spade a spade and lay it on the (7) ______ – I don't believe your story."

"OK. It's time to come (8) ______ and set the (9) ______ straight. There was no UFO. It was just a joke, but my wife thought it was (10) ______ the up and up. I don't know how to tell her the truth."

"Well, I'll make no (11) ______ about it – what you did was stupid and a waste of my time. But your wife doesn't need to know."

"You won't tell her? Thank you from the (12) ______ of my heart."

B *Scrambled sentences*

Put the words in these sentences into the correct order.

1. that something story about his rings is hollow There

   There is something about his story that rings hollow.

2. and beat They us square fair.

   ______

3. pull any The punches reporter didn't news.

   ______

4. is about on Everything level the business the.

   ______

5. bottom to to I get the of intend this.

   ______

Focus on use

A *Formality*

These sentences are from a formal letter of application. Remove the idioms in blue and rewrite the sentences to make the letter sound more formal.

Dear Sir or Madam:

I am writing to apply for the Good Student Scholarship Fund. I enclose my most recent transcripts and references.

You will see from my records that I have fulfilled the requirements for the program. My references are from two of my professors, and I think what they say about me is on the level.

1. ....

I will come clean – I have applied to the Good Student Scholarship Fund once before.

2. ....

I won't make any bones about it, I think I will do a great job if you give me the scholarship.

3. ....

Thank you from the bottom of my heart.

4. ....

B *Over to you*

*Many idioms in English related to honesty and truth use the words "**up**" or "**straight**." Think of honesty and truth idioms in your language. Are they similar to the English idioms in some way? Explain.*

Now write

Write a paragraph about something that you feel should be **taken with a grain of salt** and explain why you think so. Possible topics are a political speech, advertising claims, or descriptions of real estate.

Unit 28

Knowledge

Kim: I thought you said you knew this path like the back of your hand.

Tom: I know it inside out. It's just that I forgot to keep track of the turns. I'm a little mixed up, that's all.

Kim: I don't think you have the foggiest idea where we are or how to get back. You're out of your depth, admit it.

Tom: We're getting close – I can feel it in my bones.

Kim: Oh, sure. I'm wise to you. You don't have a clue. How you got a job as a walking guide is anybody's guess!

Tom: Ah, yes, here we are, back at camp.

Kim: Oh. You're right. Uh, sorry about what I said back there. It was a nice hike. You do know your stuff.

Knowing

- **know something inside out** to know everything about something
- **know something like the back of your hand** to be very familiar with something
- **know your stuff** to know a lot about a subject
- **in the know** having information about something
- **have something down pat** to have learned something completely
- **have your finger on the pulse (of something)** to know about the important things that are happening
- **keep abreast of (something)** to have the most recent information about something
- **keep track (of someone / something)** to know about any changes or developments
- **(be) wise to someone / something,** *also* **get wise to someone / something** to know about and not be fooled by someone or something
- **feel something in your bones** to know that something is true, although it can't be proven

Not knowing

- **(it) beats me,** *also* **what beats me is ____** *or* **it's anybody's / anyone's guess** said when someone doesn't know or understand something
- ⚠ **not have a clue,** *also* **without a clue** *or* **not have the faintest idea** *or* **not have the foggiest idea** not to have any information about something
- ⚠ **not know beans about something** not to know anything about it
- ⚠ **(be) out of your depth** not to know very much, or enough, about a subject

Focus on meaning

A *Odd one out*

Look at the idioms in 1–5 below. Two of the idioms have similar meanings, and one is different. Circle the idiom that does not belong.

1. a. be out of your depth
   b. know your stuff
   c. it beats me

2. a. be wise to someone or something
   b. feel something in your bones
   c. be out of your depth

3. a. keep track of something
   b. keep abreast of something
   c. something is anyone's guess

4. a. know something inside out
   b. be without a clue
   c. know something like the back of your hand

5. a. not have a clue
   b. not have the faintest idea
   c. be in the know

B *Sentence completion*

Use idioms from the box to complete the following sentences. You may have to change the form of some words.

finger on the pulse	like the back of your hand	the faintest idea
have something down pat	out of your depth	

1. We had a great taxi driver who knew the city like the back of his hand.
2. When it comes to computers, I'm still ______________.
3. He had practiced his presentation several times and felt that he ______________.
4. The secret of good marketing is to have your ______________ of your target market.
5. "What's her phone number?" "Sorry, I don't have ______________."

Focus on form

A *Correct or incorrect?*

Are these sentences correct? Put a check (✔) in the box if the sentence is correct. Put an ✘ in the box and correct the idiom if it is wrong.

1. Don't worry, I know this neighborhood like the back hand. ☒ Don't worry, I know this neighborhood like the back of my hand.
2. He's a great teacher. He really knows his stuff. ☐ ....
3. When the discussion turned to politics, I was out in my depth. ☐ ....
4. Liz doesn't know beans about management. ☐ ....
5. I knew something was wrong. I could touch it on my bones. ☐ ....
6. They have their thumb on the pulse of teenage fashion. ☐ ....
7. People in know say that he is guilty. ☐ ....
8. He used to go to the gym for free until the staff got wise on him. ☐ ....

B *Knowledge crossword*

Complete the crossword by filling in the missing word in each idiom.

Across

3 It ...... me! (5 letters)

6 He knows it ...... out. (6)

8 It's anyone's ...... what time they'll start. (5)

9 How do you keep ...... of everyone? (5)

Down

1 I haven't got a .... (4)

2 Don't try to sing the song until you have the words ...... pat. (4)

4 They're keeping ...... of developments. (7)

5 She's a good guide and knows her .... (5)

7 I don't have the faintest ...... where you left it.

Focus on use

A *Formality*

You are the director of a company. A new manager has written a report on someone in the department, but the language is too strong and too direct. Use the phrases in the box to replace the idioms in blue.

be an expert	know about	no one knows
I do not understand	knows nothing about	

Simon has been working here for six months. He really should know his stuff

(1) .... by now, but he does not know beans about

(2) .... the department. What beats me is

(3) .... why we did not get wise to

(4) .... this situation earlier. It's anyone's guess

(5) .... whether he will improve, but I doubt that he will.

B *Over to you*

1. *Is there a common phrase in your language that means* ***not know beans about something****? What is it?*
2. *Is there a common phrase in your language that means* ***to feel it in your bones****? What is it?*

Now write

Write about a time when you felt that you were **out of your depth** in a situation.

Unit 29

Memory

I got back from vacation and couldn't remember my computer password. I was racking my brain all morning trying to remember. It was on the tip of my tongue – I could almost remember it, but not quite.

I thought I'd committed it to memory, but I couldn't remember it at all. Nothing.

I walked around the office, looking at things and hoping something might jog my memory. I picked up a photograph of my family. Something rang a bell.

Just then the phone rang. It was my mother.

"Hi, Ed, did you stop at the store on your way to work?"

"No, it slipped my mind. What was I supposed to get? Refresh my memory."

"Cat food."

That's it! It came back to me. My password is Domino, the cat's name!

"Thanks! That's great!" I logged on.

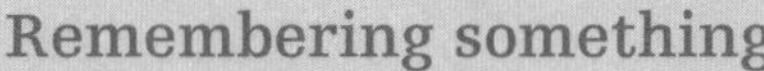

Remembering something

- **something comes back (to someone)** something is remembered by someone
- **bear something in mind,** *also* **keep something in mind** to think about or consider something as you make a decision
- **have something at the back of your mind** to know or remember something without actively considering it
- **make a mental note** to decide to remember something at some time in the future
- **rack your brain** to try very hard to remember something
- **on the tip of your tongue** almost remembered
- **ring a bell** to seem familiar
- **learn something by heart** to memorize it exactly
- **commit something to memory** to memorize something

Being reminded of something

- **bring something to mind,** *also* **call something to mind** to make you remember something
- **jog your memory** to cause you to remember something
- **take you back** to make you remember something about the past
- **refresh your memory** to remind you of information you have forgotten

Forgetting things

- **slip your mind** to forget something temporarily
- **lose track of something** to forget about something for a short period
- **your mind goes blank** you cannot remember anything

Focus on meaning

A *Matching*

Match the idioms with their definitions.

1. to commit something to memory
2. something comes back
3. something slips your mind
4. jog someone's memory
5. rack your brain
6. refresh someone's memory
7. rings a bell

a. you begin to remember something
b. to give someone information about something he or she has forgotten
c. something makes you partly remember something
d. to try hard to remember something
e. to memorize something
f. to cause someone to remember something
g. you temporarily forget something

B *Grouping*

Use the words in the box as headings for each group of idioms.

remember something	forget	cause someone to remember something
memorize	try to remember	

1. remember something
bear something in mind
bring something to mind
have something at the back of your mind

2. ....
jog someone's memory
something takes you back
refresh someone's memory

3. ....
something slips your mind
lose track of something
your mind goes blank

4. ....
commit something to memory
learn something by heart

5. ....
make a mental note
rack your brain

Focus on form

A *Prepositions and adverbs*

Use the prepositions and adverbs in the box to complete the sentences. You will need to use some of them more than once.

at	back	in	of	on	to

1. "He's a powerful player." "I'll bear that ____in____ mind when we choose the team."
2. I couldn't remember her e-mail address; then it suddenly came ________ to me.
3. Sorry I'm late. I lost track ________ the time.
4. It's a good idea to commit your PIN number ________ memory.
5. His name is ________ the tip of my tongue.
6. The smell of peanut butter cookies always brings my grandmother ________ mind.
7. His low grades were ________ the back of my mind during the interview.
8. When I hear that song, it takes me ________ to last summer.

B *Beginnings and endings*

Match the beginnings and endings of these sentences.

1. I got to the podium, and my
2. I'm sorry, our appointment completely slipped
3. What is her name? I've been racking
4. We learned the poem by
5. Maybe these photos will jog
6. Make a mental
7. "Do you know Martha?" "Well, the name
8. Let me refresh your

a. my brain trying to remember.
b. note to come back for the sale.
c. mind suddenly went blank!
d. memory.
e. rings a bell."
f. your memory.
g. my mind.
h. heart.

Focus on use

A *Politeness*

Sometimes saying something too directly sounds rude. Decide whether** a **or** b **is more polite. Circle your answer.

1. You missed an important meeting with your boss.
   a. Well, you know, everything you tell me just goes in one ear and out the other.
   b. I'm sorry. I was working on the Avery account, and I lost track of the time.

2. You see someone you have met before. You can't remember her name.
   a. Hello! Your name is on the tip of my tongue.
   b. Who are you?

3. You are speaking to an important customer. You need to remind him to pay a bill for $750.
   a. We haven't received payment for your order.
   b. Does the amount of $750 ring any bells?

4. You suddenly remember it's your partner's birthday. You call and say:
   a. Your birthday completely slipped my mind.
   b. I've been racking my brain trying to think of something to get you. Let's just go out for a nice dinner.

B *Over to you*

Answer the following questions. Use some of the idioms from this unit.

1. Do you have a good or a bad memory? Explain.

2. Have you ever been embarrassed because of something that you forgot? Tell the story of what happened.

Now write

Write a short story about a forgetful person – maybe about yourself! Use five idioms from this unit in your story.

Unit 30 Responsibility and control

Responsibility

- **carry the ball** to do the work or take the responsibility to achieve something
- **get someone off the hook**, *also* **let someone off the hook** to free someone from a responsibility or a difficult situation
- **mind the store** to be responsible for the business or organization
- **on someone's shoulders** as a personal responsibility of someone
- **step up to the plate** to take responsibility for doing something

*Young people **carried the ball** for her campaign.*

Control

- **at the helm (of something)** [slightly formal] in control
- **bend the rules** to allow something to be done that is not usually done
- **call the shots** to make the important decisions
- **get your own way** to succeed in being allowed to do what you want
- **in the driver's seat** in control of a situation
- **lay down the law** to tell people what they must do, without caring about their opinions
- **leave you to your own devices** to allow you to decide for yourself what you do
- **take on a life of its own** to no longer be controlled by anyone
- **twist someone's arm** to strongly encourage or persuade someone to do something he or she does not want to do
- **under someone's / something's thumb,** *also* **under the thumb of someone / something** completely controlled by someone or something

*Martha's **in the driver's seat** when it's time to write our report.*

Focus on meaning

A *Matching*

Find an idiom in the list below to match each definition.

Definitions

1. a personal responsibility
2. begin to take responsibility
3. cause someone to do something they don't want to do
4. completely controlled by someone or something
5. do or allow something that is not usually allowed
6. do the necessary work or take responsibility for getting something done
7. help someone avoid difficulty
8. in control
9. be responsible for a business or organization

Idioms

a. at the helm / in the driver's seat
b. bend the rules
c. carry the ball
d. get someone off the hook
e. mind the store
f. on someone's shoulders
g. step up to the plate
h. twist someone's arm
i. under someone's thumb

B *Sentence transformation*

Rewrite these sentences, using the idioms in parentheses.

1. Now that you're in management, you've got to start making the big decisions. (call / shots)

   Now that you're in management, you've got to start calling the shots.

2. Our new teacher walked in the first day and told us exactly what we had to do. (lay down / law)

3. Just let them decide for themselves. (leave / devices)

4. Once an earthquake starts, it cannot be controlled by anyone. (take / life / its own)

5. The kids always get to do what they want. (get / way)

Focus on form

A *Beginnings and endings*

Match the beginnings and endings of these idioms.

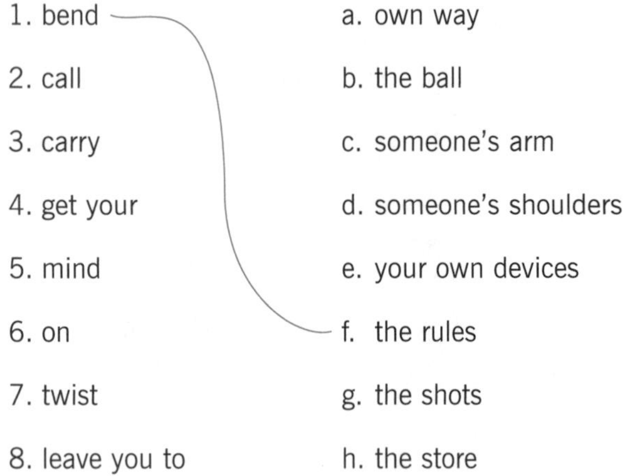

1. bend	a. own way
2. call	b. the ball
3. carry	c. someone's arm
4. get your	d. someone's shoulders
5. mind	e. your own devices
6. on	f. the rules
7. twist	g. the shots
8. leave you to	h. the store

B *Prepositions*

Use some, but not all, of the prepositions in the box to complete the sentences.

at down in of off on through to under up

1. Thanks for getting me ___off___ the hook.
2. He's been ________ his father's thumb all his life.
3. We have a new manager ________ the helm.
4. It's time you stepped ________ ________ the plate.
5. How do you like being ________ the driver's seat?
6. This project has taken ________ a life ________ its own.
7. You can't just walk in here and start laying ________ the law.

Focus on use

A *Formality*

This letter of application for a job is intended to be formal, but the writer has used some informal idioms. Replace the idioms so that the style of the letter is more appropriate.

Director
International Marketing and Sales Division
Educational Solutions

Dear Sir / Madam:

I am writing to inquire about management opportunities with Educational Solutions. I enclose a full resume. Relevant aspects of my career are highlighted below.

I am currently managing a team of six sales people at Educational Concerns. I took over this position two years ago when my manager left unexpectedly and I was asked to mind the store (1) ....

I had been in sales for three years. Although management had largely left us to our own devices (2) ...., I had no management experience. But I stepped up to the plate (3) .... and began calling the shots (4) ....

I enjoy managing a team, but I also know when to carry the ball (5) .... myself.

I look forward to hearing from you.

Sincerely,

B *Over to you*

Can you think of a situation in which it might be OK to ***bend the rules****? Explain.*

Now write

Write about a time when someone tried to **twist your arm** about a project or an event that **took on a life of its own**. The event could be something you were personally involved in or a public event.

Unit 31

Risks and opportunities

Bob used to be a rich man, but he tempted fate once too often and now he's bankrupt.

He would listen to anyone with a new idea. People knew that once they got their foot in the door with Bob, he would jump at the chance to invest. He always wanted to have the first crack at a deal.

He was willing to stick his neck out because he didn't want to miss the boat. Sometimes the ideas were risky but good, sometimes crazy. But he usually had plenty of projects, so it didn't really matter if one or two failed.

Then he put all his eggs in one basket and lost everything. He should have played it safe.

Taking risks and chances

- **bet the farm**, *also* **bet the ranch** to risk everything because you are certain of something
- **go for broke** to risk everything and try as hard as possible to achieve something
- **put all your eggs in one basket** to risk everything in support of one idea or plan
- **tempt fate** to take a foolish or unnecessary risk
- **stick your neck out** to take a risk even though it might cause problems for you
- **put your life on the line** to risk dying
- **play it safe** to avoid risks

Having opportunities

- **get your foot in the door** to have an opportunity to do or be involved in something for the first time
- **given half a chance** allowed an opportunity
- **have (the) first crack at something** to be the first one to have an opportunity to do something
- **jump at the chance** to accept an opportunity quickly and eagerly

Missing opportunities

- **let something slip through your fingers** to waste an opportunity to do something
- **miss the boat** to lose an opportunity
- **(be) out of luck** not to have an opportunity to do something
- **pass up something**, *also* **pass something up** to fail to take an opportunity

Focus on meaning

Concept map

Complete this concept map, using the idioms in the box.

a. bet the farm / ranch
b. get your foot in the door
c. go for broke
d. have (the) first crack at something
e. jump at the chance
f. let something slip through your fingers
g. miss the boat
h. out of luck
i. play it safe
j. put all your eggs in one basket
k. put your life on the line
l. stick your neck out
m. tempt fate
n. pass up something

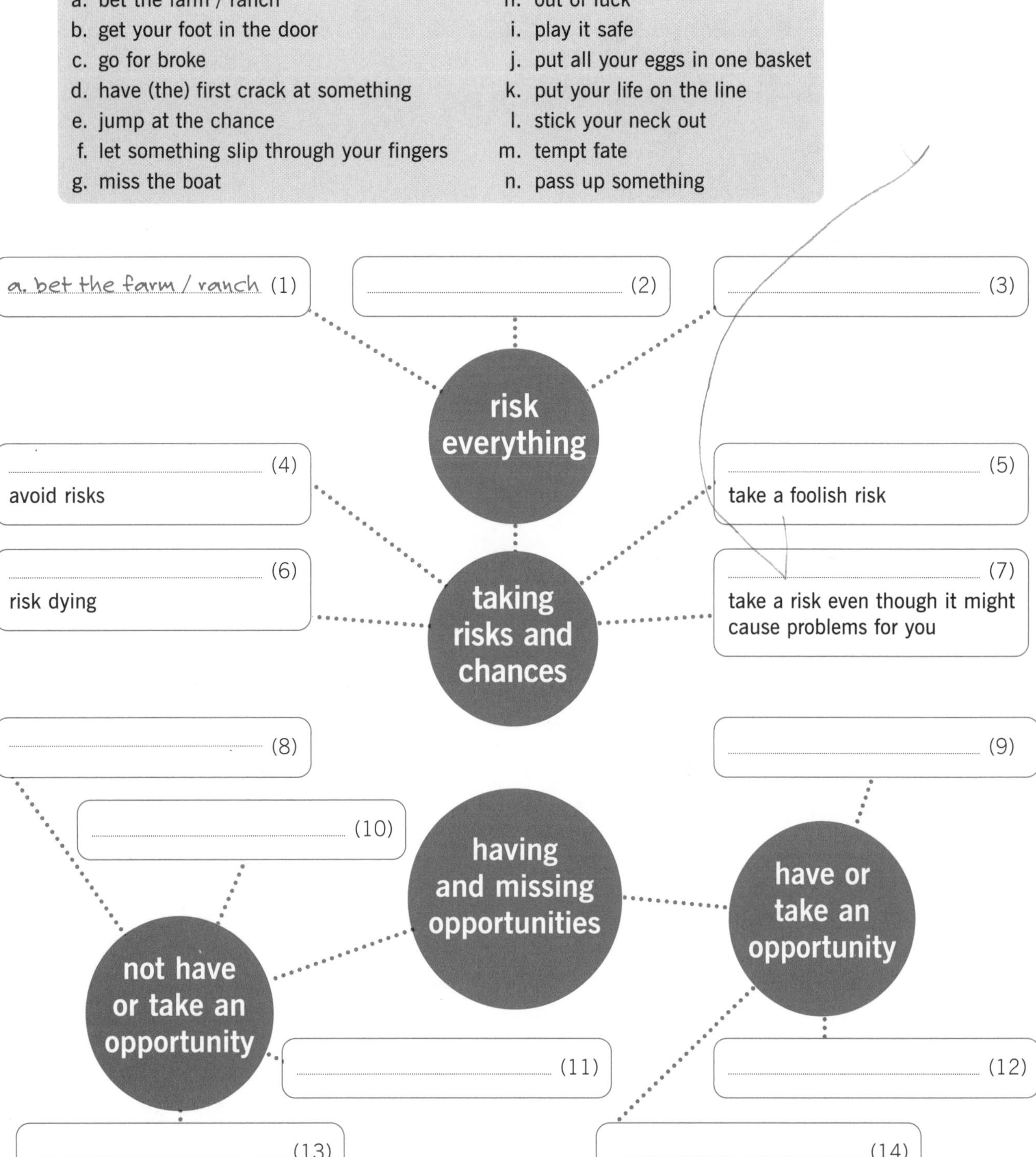

Focus on form

A *Prepositions*

Use the prepositions in the box to complete the sentences. You will need to use some of the prepositions more than once.

at	for	in	on	out	through

1. I met the managing director. I think I've got my foot ____in____ the door.
2. I say let's go ________ broke!
3. We should let them have first crack ________ this project.
4. Don't be silly and put all your eggs ________ one basket.
5. He's not willing to stick his neck ________.
6. I know he'd put his life ________ the line for a friend.
7. You can't let opportunities like this slip ________ your fingers.
8. You're ________ of luck, I'm afraid.

B *Scrambled sentences*

Put the words in these sentences into the correct order.

1. play Dad thinks I it safe should. ____Dad thinks I should play it safe.____
2. bet Don't ranch the! ________
3. tempting think you're I fate. ________
4. boat today Reply that the you don't so miss. ________
5. chance win, half a We'll given. ________
6. your Would neck for this stick out you deal? ________
7. luck this out of time You're. ________
8. at jump I'd chance the! ________

Focus on use

A *Risk questionnaire*

Are you a risk taker? Circle the letters of your answers and then check your score on page 201.

1. You get a big bonus at work. Do you . . . ?
   a. play it safe and put it in the bank
   b. invest it in a company you know well
   c. go for broke and bet it all on a horse race

2. You have the first crack at investing in a new media company. Do you . . . ?
   a. read everything you can about the company and the market before doing anything
   b. discuss the project, then invest moderately
   c. jump at the chance and hope everything works out

3. You have been trying to get your foot in the door of a company. You are introduced to the CEO at a party. She gives you her card. Do you . . . ?
   a. take the card and think about writing to her later
   b. ask her if you can send her a resume
   c. stick your neck out and ask for an appointment right then

4. You're a rock musician but you haven't been able to get a record deal. You are working as a waiter at a party at a record company. Do you . . . ?
   a. decide not to say anything at the party but remember a few names and call those people next week
   b. introduce yourself to one of the junior staff members and ask if you can send a demo disk
   c. jump up on the stage before the band comes on and play one of your own songs

B *Over to you*

Are there common phrases in your language that mean the same as ***miss the boat*** *or* ***jump at the chance****? What are they?*

Now write

Write a paragraph about a time in your life when you either **played it safe** and later wished you had been more daring, or decided to **go for broke** and later wished you'd been more careful.

Unit 32

Strength and weakness

Strength

- **a pillar of strength** someone who is emotionally strong
- **(as) strong as an ox,** *also* **(as) strong as a bull** very strong
- **(as) tough as nails,** *also* **(as) hard as nails** strong and determined
- **come on strong** to act in a forceful way
- **flex your / its muscles** to act in a way that shows power or strength
- **make your presence felt** to have a strong effect on other people or on a situation
- **prove your mettle** *also* **show your mettle** [slightly formal], to show that you are brave and have a strong character
- **tough it out** to be strong while experiencing difficulties
- **beef up something,** *also* **beef something up** to make something stronger or more effective
- **a shot in the arm** a strong positive influence

*Conservatives are **flexing their muscles** in local elections this fall.*

- **get a second wind,** *also* **get your / its second wind** to have increased energy or strength after feeling tired or weak
- **mind over matter** thought is stronger than physical things

Weakness

- **a shadow of your / its former self** a smaller, weaker, or less important form of someone or something
- **take advantage (of someone)** to use someone's weakness to improve your own situation
- **a house of cards** an organization or a plan that is very weak and can easily be destroyed

*Their partners began to suspect that the company was a financial **house of cards**.*

Focus on meaning

A *Physical or mental?*

Are these idioms used mainly to describe physical strength and weakness or mental / emotional strength or weakness? Put the idioms in the correct column.

a. a pillar of strength
b. a shadow of your former self
c. a shot in the arm
d. as strong as an ox
e. mind over matter
f. prove or show your mettle

Physical strength or weakness	Mental / emotional strength or weakness
b. shadow of your former self	

B *Correct or incorrect*

Below each numbered sentence is a restatement of it. Put a check (✔) in the box if it is correct. If it is incorrect, put an ✘ in the box and correct it.

1. The industry has gotten a second wind. ☑ ______
   The industry is strong again.
2. This nation is beginning to flex its muscles as a producer of coffee. ☐ ______
   This country is showing that it is a producer of coffee.
3. The peace agreement is a house of cards. ☐ ______
   We think the agreement will succeed.
4. I didn't want to come on too strong, so I tried not to seem angry. ☐ ______
   I wanted to appear weak, so I tried not to seem angry.
5. They take advantage of part-time teachers. ☐ ______
   Part-time teachers do well.
6. We need to beef up the proposal. ☐ ______
   We need to strengthen the proposal.
7. I suggest you try to tough it out. ☐ ______
   I suggest you give up.
8. Their team was hard as nails. ☐ ______
   Their team was very flexible.

Focus on form

A *Odd one out – pronunciation*

Look at the groups of words below each idiom. One has a vowel sound that is similar to the word from the idiom; the other is different. Circle the word that does not belong.

1. **as tough as nails / tough it out**

   tough: a. though
   b. stuff

2. **a shot in the arm**

   shot: a. plot
   b. show

3. **get a second wind**

   wind: a. kind
   b. hit

4. **prove your mettle**

   prove: a. spoon
   b. love

5. **mind over matter**

   mind: a. mint
   b. kind

6. **beef something up**

   beef: a. been
   b. piece

B *Beginnings and endings*

Match the beginnings and endings of these idioms.

1. a house of	a. advantage of someone
2. a pillar of	b. your former self
3. a shadow of	c. your presence felt
4. as strong as	d. your muscles
5. come on	e. strength
6. flex	f. an ox
7. make	g. strong
8. take	h. cards

Focus on use

A *What do you say?*

Using idioms from the unit, what could you say in these situations?

1. You recently experienced a very difficult time. Someone you work with was very supportive through your problems. You want to thank the person.
2. Your friend has just been elected to the Student Council but is a bit shy in meetings.
3. You are a musician. You were about to give up making music. Then someone wrote a really good review of one of your concerts, and it encouraged you to make a demo. Now you are famous and want to thank that person.
4. You and a friend are lost in the jungle. You have run out of food, but you must keep going.

B *Over to you*

Can you think of idioms in your language that have similar meanings to these?

1. as strong as an ox
2. as tough as nails
3. a shadow of your former self
4. mind over matter

Now write

Think either about a time when someone has been a **pillar of strength** for you or about a time when someone has given you a **shot in the arm**. Write about what happened and how you felt.

Unit 33

Success

- **bring off something**, *also* **bring something off** *or* **carry off something** *or* **carry something off** *or* **hit a home run** to succeed in doing something
- **hit pay dirt**, *also* **strike pay dirt** *or* **hit the jackpot** to succeed
- **carry the day** to win or succeed
- **sail through something** to succeed easily in something
- **take off** to succeed suddenly
- **have the last laugh** to succeed in the end, especially when others thought you would not

Julie ***carried the day*** *and came home with three first prizes.*

- **make a go of something**, *also* **make a go of it** to try to succeed in an activity, *also* to try to make a relationship succeed
- **make good** to become successful
- **scrape by** to come very close to failing

When we saw the newspapers the next morning, we knew we had ***hit a home run****.*

- **win out** to succeed after great effort
- **have a good run**, *also* **have a great run** to experience success
- **pull off something**, *also* **pull something off** to succeed in doing something difficult or unexpected

The company fired her, but she ***had the last laugh:*** *she was hired by its main rival at twice the salary.*

Focus on meaning

A *Matching*

These idioms all mean "to succeed," but they are slightly different from each other. Match each idiom with its meaning.

To succeed . . .	Idioms
1. as a result of great effort	a. sail through something
2. in doing something difficult or unexpected	b. take off
3. easily	c. have the last laugh
4. nearly fail	d. pull something off
5. when others think you will not	e. scrape by
6. suddenly	f. win out

B *Odd one out*

Look at the idioms in 1–4 below. Two of the idioms have similar meanings, and one is slightly different. Circle the idiom that does not belong.

1. a. hit pay dirt
   b. make good
   c. hit the jackpot
2. a. hit a home run
   b. have a good run
   c. hit the jackpot
3. a. hit a home run
   b. hit pay dirt
   c. make a go
4. a. carry something off
   b. scrape by
   c. carry the day

*He was the local boy who **made good** in Hollywood.*

Focus on form

A *Prepositions and adverbs*

Use the prepositions and adverbs in the box to complete the sentences. You will need to use some of them more than once.

by	off	out	through

1. Only a very large company has the resources to bring ____off____ this kind of deal.
2. In the end, our hard work won ________.
3. She never lies, because she doesn't have a good enough memory to carry it ________.
4. Jess sailed ________ the election and is the new president of the Student Council.
5. The style really took ________ among teens.
6. I don't know how you pulled it ________.
7. He just scraped ________ and made it into the finals.

B *Beginnings and endings*

Match the beginnings and endings of these sentences.

Beginnings	Endings
1. The family moved away and made	a. jackpot this time!
2. I'm willing to try and make	b. home run every time.
3. You can't expect to hit a	c. good in their new home.
4. I've had a great	d. day and won every race.
5. We really hit the	e. last laugh.
6. Don't worry. We'll have the	f. a go of it, if you are.
7. James carried the	g. pay dirt.
8. We got lucky and hit	h. run and I've enjoyed every minute of it.

Focus on use

A *What do you say?*

Which idioms would you use in the following situations?

1. Your friend wrote a children's book that no one would publish. Now it's being made into a Hollywood movie.
2. Someone asks you about your driver's test. It went very well.
3. Your friend won a scholarship – there were a lot of good candidates.
4. Your brother is starting his senior year of high school. He wants to go to college, but he almost failed three classes in his junior year.
5. A coworker is thinking about going into business for him/herself. You think he/she will do well.
6. You are reporting back to your boss about a very successful sales trip.

B *Over to you*

*In your language, are there idioms about success that come from games, like **hit a home run** or **hit the jackpot**? What are they?*

Now write

Write a paragraph about a time in your life when you really had to work hard to succeed, or about a time when you came close to failing to do something. Use some of the idioms from the unit.

Unit 34 Value

Message Board

Alex: I'm thinking about dropping out of college and buying a degree online. I want to make sure I get my money's worth.

Buddy: The package from Digital Degrees offers the best bang for your buck. The beauty of it is, if you buy an MA and a PhD, you get a free BA!

Alex: Wow, that sounds great.

Buddy: It costs a little more than the standard MA/PhD package, but it's well worth it.

Carl: Wait a minute, Alex, I got one of those packages – the degrees are not worth the paper they're printed on. Employers know all about these fake degrees and really look down on them. Besides, it's not just the degree – the whole college experience is well worth it. I took a lot of things for granted when I was at college. You'll appreciate it in the end.

Valuable

- **bang for the buck,** *also* **bang for your buck** value in exchange for money or effort
- **the beauty of something** a quality that makes something good, easy, or of value
- **(it's well) worth it** it is rewarding despite the difficulties involved
- **get your money's worth** [especially spoken] to receive good value for the amount you have paid
- ⚠ **worth a damn** [especially spoken] to have value (usually used in a negative form)

Not valuable, worthless

- **look down on someone / something,** *also* **look down your nose at someone / something** to consider someone or something as not important or of value
- **make a mockery of something** to make something seem stupid or without value
- **not worth the paper something is printed on** to have no value or importance
- **take someone / something for granted** to fail to appreciate the value of someone or something

To become valuable

- **pick up speed** to increase in value or degree

To lose value

- **go south** lose value or quality
- **the bottom fell out (of something)** something suddenly lost value

Focus on meaning

Sentence transformation

Rewrite these sentences, using the idioms suggested by the clues in parentheses.

1. This is a great little camera that gives you value for money. (bang)

   This is a great little camera that gives you bang for your buck.

2. I spend so much on repairs, I wonder if I paid too much for it. (worth)

3. When the real estate market suddenly lost value, a lot of people lost a lot of money. (bottom)

4. She decided to sell her stocks because she felt the market was losing value. (south)

5. Stocks increased in value in the final hour of trading this afternoon. (speed)

6. So many of us don't realize how lucky we are to have clean water. (granted)

7. The landlord's promises are totally worthless. (paper)

8. The case made the legal process look worthless. (mockery)

9. Some people think that the homeless are worthless. (look)

10. The good thing about the Internet is its openness. (beauty)

11. Kids in this city aren't getting an education that has much value. (damn)

12. It was a long climb up the hill, but the view from the top was rewarding. (worth)

13. When you're a kid, you don't appreciate your parents. (granted)

Focus on form

A *Correct or incorrect?*

Are these sentences correct? Some have an extra word. Put a check (✔) in the box if the sentence is correct. Put an ✘ in the box and circle the extra word if it is wrong.

1. Several key people resigned, and the company went (down) south. ☒
2. We sold our house before the bottom fell out of the property market. ☐
3. Retail sales picked up to speed just before the holidays. ☐
4. It's well the worth booking in advance. ☐
5. Some teachers look far down on electronic dictionaries. ☐

B *Spell check*

Choose the correct spelling.

1. This law makes a ______ of free speech.
   a. mockerey (b. mockery) c. mockeries
2. This contract is not ______ the paper it's printed on.
   a. worth b. worse c. wearth
3. The ______ of this contest is that anyone can enter.
   a. beauties b. beuaty c. beauty
4. You get a lot more ______ for your buck when you shop online.
   a. bang b. bangs c. bank
5. She has always taken him for ______ .
   a. grant b. granite c. granted
6. His research isn't ______ a ______.
   a. worse / damn b. worthe / danm c. worth / damn
7. Are you getting your money's ______?
   a. worth b. worse c. wouth
8. The ______ may fall out of the market.
   a. butter b. button c. bottom

Focus on use

A *Virus alert!*

You write a financial column for In the Know News. *A computer virus wiped out all the idioms in your latest column. Put them back in.*

In the Know News

Last week I told you that if you wanted maximum **(1)** ...., you should invest in Small Fortune Hotels, because it seemed to be **(2)** .... That has all changed now, since the **(3)** .... the travel industry over the weekend.

I am sorry if you bought stocks in the company. They are **(4)** .... now.

B *Over to you*

Proverbs are common sayings. Look at these proverbs, in English, about value:

a. All that glitters is not gold.
b. A bird in the hand is worth two in the bush.
c. Don't count your chickens before they hatch.
d. Don't put all your eggs in one basket.

1. What do they mean?
2. Are there similar sayings in your language?

Now write

Write about one of the following topics.

1. Something that you have done that was difficult but was **well worth it**
2. Things that we **take for granted** that may not be available ten years from now

Unit 35

Animals

- **someone / something has more bark than bite,** *also* **someone's bark is worse than his / her bite** *or* **something's bark is worse than its bite** something is not as unpleasant as you expected
- **a bird's-eye view** the appearance of something seen from above, or a general view of something
- **beat a dead horse** to waste time trying to do something that will not succeed
- **call off the dogs,** *also* **call off your dogs** to cause people to stop attacking or criticizing someone
- **fish or cut bait** either to act or to decide you are not going to do anything
- ⚠ **for the birds** without value
- **get off your high horse** to stop acting as if you are better or more intelligent than other people

Get off your high horse *and go out there and talk to them.*

- **let the cat out of the bag** to tell something that is a secret, often without intending to
- **(put) the cart before the horse** to do something that should happen after other things
- **(straight) from the horse's mouth** from someone who has the facts
- **take the bull by the horns** to deal directly with someone or something

It's time to ***fish or cut bait*** *– stop talking about buying it and write the check!*

- ⚠ **go to the dogs** to become worse in quality or character
- **have bigger fish to fry,** *also* **have other fish to fry** to have something more important or more interesting to do
- **horse around** to be active in a silly way
- **in the doghouse** in a situation in which someone is annoyed with you because of something you did

Stop ***horsing around*** *and get to bed!*

Focus on meaning

Sentence completion

Use idioms from the box to complete the following sentences. You may have to change the form of some words.

beating a dead horse	gone to the dogs	let the cat out of the bag
bird's-eye view	got off his high horse	putting the cart before the horse
call off the dogs	his bark is worse than his bite	other fish to fry
fish or cut bait	horsing around	straight from the horse's mouth
for the birds	in the doghouse	took the bull by the horns

1. "Are you sure she's leaving?" "Definitely, I heard it straight from the horse's mouth."
2. "What do you think of the new system?" "I think it's ______ – it won't work."
3. Amazingly, not one of the people who knew about the surprise ______.
4. Do you think it's worth sending my manuscript to other publishers, or am I just ______?
5. He never ______ long enough to consider how insulting his words were to many immigrants.
6. He sounds tough, but ______.
7. I couldn't spend a lot of time on the problem – I had ______.
8. I ______ and confronted him about his smoking.
9. It is sad to report that this once first-class hotel has ______.
10. It's time to ______ and let her get back to doing her job.
11. Stop ______ and pay attention to your father!
12. The city is ______ by building a stadium before a team has agreed to play here.
13. The large painting offers a ______ that shows the layout of the ancient city.
14. The president's aide is ______ over remarks he made to the press.
15. The time has come when you have to ______ – either you help us plan what to do or we will decide and go ahead without you.

Focus on form

A *Beginnings and endings*

Match the beginnings and endings of these idioms.

1. more bark	a. before the horse
2. a bird's-	b. than bite
3. call off	c. high horse
4. fish or	d. fish to fry
5. get off your	e. eye view
6. go to the	f. by the horns
7. have bigger	g. doghouse
8. in the	h. cut bait
9. (put) the cart	i. the dogs
10. take the bull	j. dogs

B *Pronunciation*

Complete this poem with idioms from the box.

beating a dead horse	for the birds	straight from the horse's mouth
the cat is out of the bag	got other fish to fry	

I spent the best years of my life
beating a dead horse (1)
You never really loved me –
I should have known, of course!

Now that .... (2)
I'm not even going to cry
I've met somebody new
And I've .... (3)

I'm not wasting any more time
Not listening to your empty words
What we had was nothing –
It was strictly .... (4)!

So my new love and I are leaving
We're going to drive down south.
I never loved you either – you heard it
.... (5)

Focus on use

A *What's your advice?*

What advice would you give to the people in each of the situations below? Use idioms from the box.

a. fish or cut bait	c. take the bull by the horns
b. get off your high horse	

1. I don't know what to do. I'm really worried about his smoking. I'm afraid to say anything . . .
2. We're thinking about taking a year off and going around the world. We're not getting any younger.
3. Several of the families in our neighborhood want to have a street party to raise money for the local school. This is a good neighborhood. Street parties are disgusting.

B *Over to you*

Can you think of animal idioms in your language that are similar to the idioms in this unit? What are they?

Now write

Think of a serious problem in the world today. Write a paragraph explaining how that problem could be solved or improved. Use two or three idioms from the unit.

Unit 36

Colors

Red / rose / pink

- **in the red** spending more money than you are earning
- **roll out the red carpet (for someone)** to give a special welcome to someone important
- **paint the town red** to go out and celebrate without control
- **(look) through rose-colored glasses** think that things are better than they really are
- **see red** to become very angry
- **in the pink** very strong and operating well

*We had a great time – they really **rolled out the red carpet for us**.*

Black (and white)

- **black and white** a very clear choice that causes no confusion
- **black out** to stop being conscious
- **in black and white** in written or printed form
- **in the black** earning more money than you are spending
- **the pot calling the kettle black** to criticize another person for a fault that you have yourself

*He hasn't had a job in years, and he said he thought they were lazy – talk about **the pot calling the kettle black**!*

Green

- **give someone / something the green light,** *also* **give the green light to someone / something** to give permission for something to happen
- **green with envy** wishing very much that you had what someone else has

*Libby's trip across Australia sounded wonderful – and we were **green with envy**.*

Blue

- **out of the blue,** *also* **out of a clear blue sky** happening suddenly and unexpectedly
- **until you are blue in the face** for a long time
- **a bolt from the blue** something sudden and unexpected

*We played music for years, and then, like a **bolt from the blue**, we got a record deal.*

Focus on meaning

A *In other words*

Circle the statement that has the same meaning as the first sentence.

1. We got the green light on the project yesterday.
   a. We can continue with the project.
   b. We don't know whether we can continue the project or not.
2. He always sees the future through rose-colored glasses.
   a. He has a positive view of the future.
   b. He has a negative view of the future.
3. We are in the red for the third year in a row.
   a. We have extra money.
   b. We don't have enough money.
4. It's all here in black and white – $5000 now and $5000 when the job is finished.
   a. It is in writing.
   b. It is clear.
5. We argued until we were both blue in the face.
   a. We argued suddenly.
   b. We argued for a long time.
6. We should roll out the red carpet for them.
   a. We should celebrate with them.
   b. We should give them a special welcome.
7. It always makes him see red.
   a. It makes him angry.
   b. It makes him feel healthy.

B *Sentence completion*

Use idioms from the box to complete the following sentences. You may have to change the form of some words.

a bolt from the blue	in the black	paint the town red
black out	in the pink	the pot calling the kettle black
green with envy	out of the blue	

1. I don't know what happened next; I blacked out.
2. You won! Let's go out and ________.
3. Business is good, and we're back ________.
4. Ever since I heard about her new car, I've been ________.
5. You're saying they're rude? That's ________.
6. The unexpected award was ________.
7. Dad's out of the hospital and ________.
8. No one had heard of the team before they came ________.

Focus on form

A *Which color – black, blue, green, or red?*

Fill in the blanks by writing the correct color to complete the idioms.

1. Her doctor says the condition caused her to black out.
2. The news was a bolt from the ________.
3. I'll be happy when I see it in ________ and white.
4. They complained until they were both ________ in the face.
5. Roll out the ________ carpet!
6. We can't afford it – we're in the ________.
7. Now I'm going to take you out and we are going to paint the town ________.
8. She was ________ with envy.

B *Colors crossword*

Complete the crossword by filling in the missing word in each idiom.

Across

4 through rose-colored ____ (7)

6 in ____ pink *or* in ____ black (3)

Down

1 black and ____ (5)

2 give the green ____ (5)

3 the pot calling the kettle ____ (5)

5 ____ red (3)

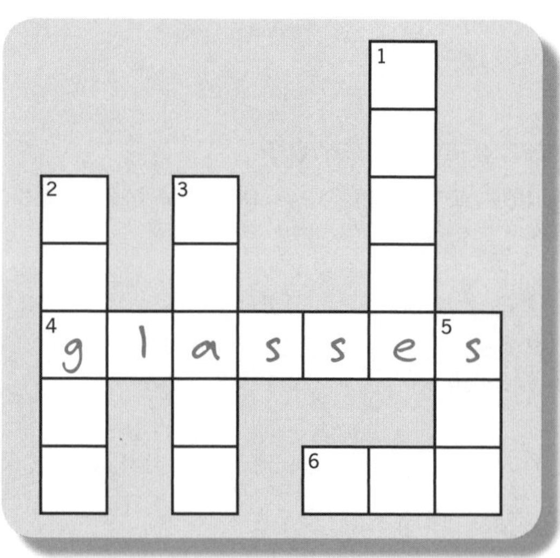

Focus on use

A *What do you say?*

Using idioms from the box, what could you say in these situations?

through rose-colored glasses	paint the town red
out of the blue / like a bolt from the blue	in black and white

1. Poor Fred. He really didn't expect it all to turn out like this. He thought everything was going to be fine.
2. Congratulations! That's great news. What would you like to do?
3. Is it true that you didn't expect the promotion?
4. I'm flying out to start my new job next week. I still haven't got a contract.

B *Over to you*

Here is a list of colors and the feelings or ideas associated with them in English. What feelings or ideas are associated with these colors in your language?

Color	Associations in English	Associations in your language
black	seriousness	
blue	sadness	
green	envy, nature, inexperience	
red	anger, danger	
white	purity, surrender	
yellow	cowardice	

Now write

Choose one of the topics below and describe it in a paragraph.

1. something that happened to you that was like **a bolt from the blue**
2. someone you know who looks at things **through rose-colored glasses**
3. someone you would **roll out the red carpet** for – and why
4. something or someone that made you **green with envy**

Unit 37

Fire and smoke

Fire

- **add fuel to the fire** make a situation worse than it already is
- **burn your fingers,** *also* **get your fingers burned** to have a bad result from something, especially to lose money
- **fan the flames (of something)** to make a bad situation worse
- **fight fire with fire** to deal with someone in the way the person is dealing with you
- **go down in flames,** *also* **go up in flames** to fail or end suddenly and completely

She's ***playing with fire*** *– he's no good.*

It's time someone ***lit a fire under the sales clerks.***

- **hold someone's feet to the fire,** *also* **put someone's feet to the fire** to cause someone to feel pressure or stress
- **light a fire under someone** to make someone work harder or better
- **out of the frying pan (into the fire)** from a bad situation to an even worse one
- **play with fire** to do something that could cause you trouble later on
- **several irons in the fire** a number of jobs or possibilities available at the same time
- **set the world on fire** to be very exciting or successful

Smoke

- ⚠ **blow smoke** to deceive others
- **go up in smoke** to be wasted
- ⚠ **smoke and mirrors** something that is meant to confuse or deceive people
- **smoke someone out** to force someone to stop hiding
- **where there's smoke, there's fire** if it looks as if something is wrong, something probably is wrong

Years of training ***went up in smoke*** *when Jake broke his leg.*

Focus on meaning

Matching

Match the idioms with their definitions.

1. add fuel to the fire
2. blow smoke
3. burn your fingers / get your fingers burned
4. fan the flames (of something)
5. fight fire with fire
6. go down in flames
7. go up in smoke
8. hold someone's feet to the fire
9. light a fire under someone
10. out of the frying pan (into the fire)
11. play with fire
12. set the world on fire
13. several irons in the fire
14. smoke and mirrors
15. smoke someone out
16. where there's smoke, there's fire

a. a number of jobs or possibilities available at the same time
b. do something that could cause you trouble later on
c. go from a bad situation to an even worse one
d. if it looks as if something is wrong, something probably is wrong
e. something that is meant to confuse or deceive people
f. to be very exciting or successful
g. to cause someone to feel pressure or stress
h. to be wasted
i. to deal with someone in the way he or she is dealing with you
j. to deceive others
k. to fail or end suddenly and completely
l. to force someone to stop hiding
m. to have a bad result from something, especially to lose money
n. to make a bad situation worse
o. to make a situation worse than it already is
p. to make someone work harder or better

Focus on form

A *Prepositions*

Use the prepositions in the box to complete the sentences. You will need to use some of the prepositions more than once.

in	into	on	out	under	up	with

1. It was ....out.......... of the frying pan and ....into.......... the fire!
2. You know you're playing .... fire.
3. We just had to sit there and watch five years' work go .... smoke.
4. I hope you've got several irons .... the fire.
5. She was only twenty-three when she set the world .... fire.
6. I think you should fight fire .... fire.
7. He's been working a lot harder since the boss lit a fire .... him.
8. It took a long time, but they finally smoked .... the terrorists.

B *Sentence completion*

Complete these sentences, using a verb or a noun. Use the correct forms.

1. Raising taxes has ....added.......... fuel to the fire.
2. The interviewer .... the politician's feet to the fire.
3. They .... their fingers on one bad deal after the other.
4. You're not helping. You're .... the flames!
5. It's all .... and mirrors.
6. The stories were true – where there's ...., there's ....
7. He was just .... smoke.
8. The conference plans ....up in flames at the last minute.

Focus on use

A *Formality*

This e-mail from Jack to his friend Charlie sounds too formal. Replace the words in blue with idioms from the box to make it sound more natural. You will need to change the form of some words.

blow smoke	hold someone's feet to the fire
(go) out of the frying pan into the fire	light a fire under someone
go up in smoke	several irons in the fire

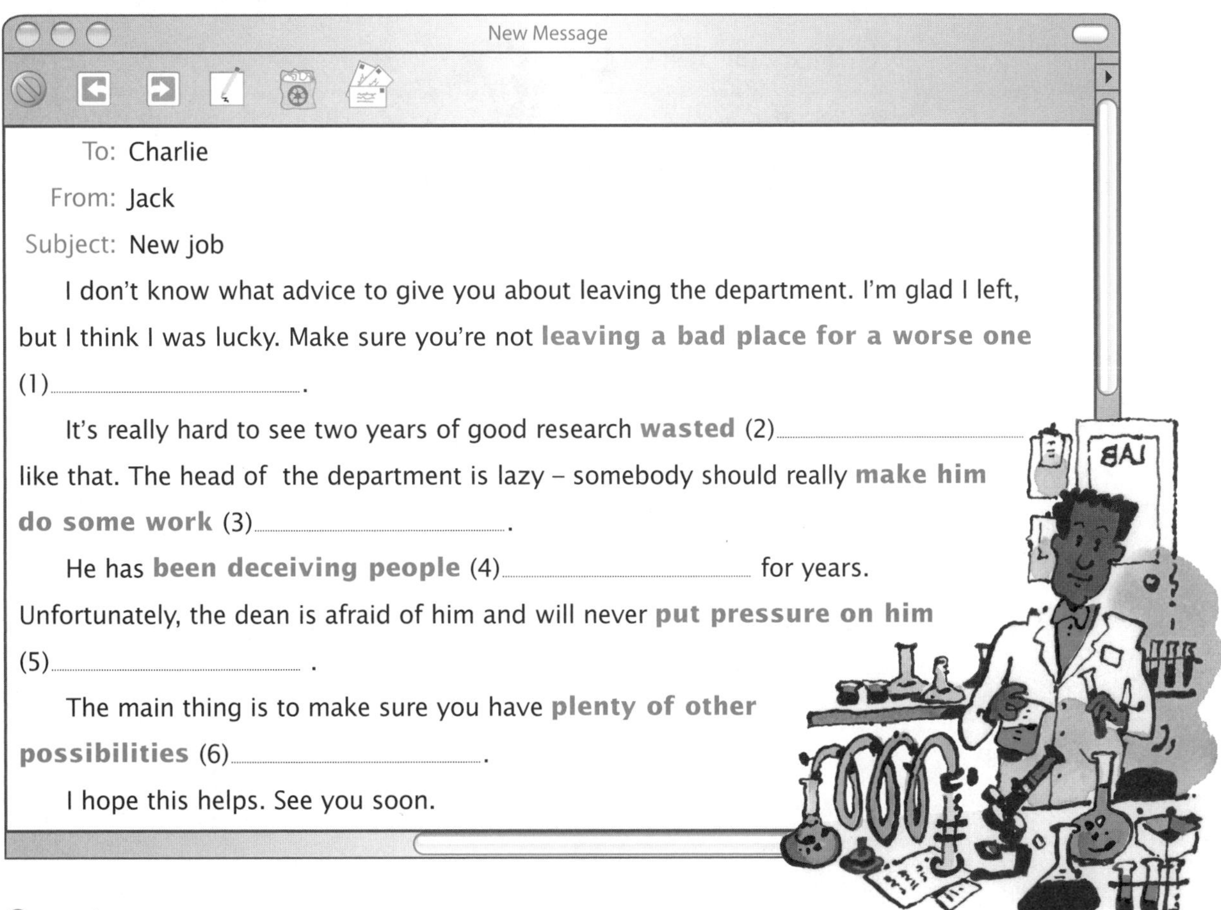

New Message

To: Charlie

From: Jack

Subject: New job

I don't know what advice to give you about leaving the department. I'm glad I left, but I think I was lucky. Make sure you're not **leaving a bad place for a worse one** (1)................................ .

It's really hard to see two years of good research **wasted** (2)................................ like that. The head of the department is lazy – somebody should really **make him do some work** (3)................................ .

He has **been deceiving people** (4)................................ for years. Unfortunately, the dean is afraid of him and will never **put pressure on him** (5)................................ .

The main thing is to make sure you have **plenty of other possibilities** (6)................................ .

I hope this helps. See you soon.

B *Over to you*

What are some "fire" or "smoke" idioms in your language? What do they mean? Are any similar to the idioms in this unit?

Now write

Write a paragraph about one of the following:

1. a time when you wish you'd had **several irons in the fire**
2. someone you knew who went **out of the frying pan into the fire**

Unit 38

Hands and shoulders

a shoulder to cry on

at first hand

give someone a hand

go hand in hand

have your hands full

(give a) thumbs down to someone

lend someone a hand

stick out *or* stand out like a sore thumb

stand shoulder to shoulder

fall into someone's hands

have a hand in doing something

wait on someone hand and foot

keep your hand in (something)

(give a) thumbs up to someone

wash your hands of someone

try your hand at something

Hands

- **at first hand** from seeing or experiencing directly
- **fall into someone's hands** to be caught or controlled by someone
- **give someone a hand,** *also* **give a hand to someone** to help someone
- **have a hand in doing something** to take part in an activity
- **go hand in hand** to be present together
- **have your hands full** to be very busy
- **keep your hand in (something)** to continue to be involved in something
- **(give a) thumbs down to someone / something** to show disapproval of or opposition to something
- **(give a) thumbs up to someone / something** to show approval of or support something
- **lend a (helping) hand,** *also* **lend someone a hand** to help do something
- **stick out like a sore thumb,** *also* **stand out like a sore thumb** to be easily noticed as different
- **try your hand at something** to attempt to do something
- **wait on someone hand and foot** to do everything for another person
- **wash your hands of someone / something** to end all involvement with someone or something

Shoulders

- **a shoulder to cry on** someone who gives you sympathy when you are upset
- **stand shoulder to shoulder** to support one another during a difficult time

Focus on meaning

A *Beginnings and endings*

Match the beginnings and endings of these sentences.

1. The whole town stood shoulder to shoulder
2. He worked as a journalist, and he also
3. You should do some of the work around here
4. If you wear jeans to the party,
5. He expected his children to
6. He was angry, and she was afraid that
7. My husband gave a big thumbs down
8. If you have any trouble with your homework,
9. He has retired, but he comes in Fridays
10. She has her hands full
11. The army was worried that weapons might fall
12. We don't put our label on anything unless
13. My father had just died, and I needed
14. Experience and ability don't always
15. It was a chance to see at first

a. you'll stand out like a sore thumb.
b. after the earthquake.
c. lend a hand where they were needed.
d. tried his hand at writing fiction.
e. instead of being waited on hand and foot all the time.
f. I'll be glad to give you a hand.
g. he would wash his hands of her.
h. to my idea of getting a new car.
i. we have a hand in designing it.
j. into rebel hands.
k. to keep his hand in.
l. raising eight children.
m. go hand in hand.
n. hand how the project was going.
o. a shoulder to cry on.

B *Sentence completion*

Use idioms from the box to complete the following sentences. You may have to change the form of some words.

give someone a hand	have your hands full
have a hand in doing something	thumbs up

1. Can you give me a hand ?
2. We were happy because the project got a ____________.
3. I'd like to thank everyone who ____________ planning this event.
4. I'm sorry I can't help you – I've really ____________.

Focus on form

A *Hands and shoulders crossword*

Complete the crossword by filling in the missing word in each idiom.

Across

2 stick out like a .... thumb (4)

3 .... on someone hand and foot (4)

5 .... a hand (4)

6 .... your hand in something (4)

7 .... your hands of something / someone (4)

Down

1 a .... to cry on (8)

2 .... shoulder to shoulder (5)

4 give something the .... up (6)

8 try your hand .... something (2)

		1			2 s	o	r	e
				3			4	
		5						
6								
					7	8		

B *Correct or incorrect?*

Are these sentences correct? Some have an extra word. Put a check (✔) in the box if the sentence is correct. Put an ✘ in the box and circle the extra word if it is wrong.

1. Give Mom a hand while I wash the dishes. ☑
2. Make sure it doesn't fall into the wrong of hands. ☐
3. They've got their hands full with all those orders. ☐
4. It's fantastic. Has Paul had a hand in this project? ☐
5. Money and good sense don't always go hand in a hand. ☐
6. Listen to the whole song before you give it a thumbs down. ☐
7. It is important to experience something like this at the first hand. ☐

Focus on use

A *What do you say?*

Using idioms from the unit, how would you respond to the following comments and questions?

1. I'm never going to finish all this work in time.
2. I'm so upset. I don't know what to do.
3. I'd like to do some painting, but I don't know whether I'd be any good at it.
4. Will your department support us if we take this to court?
5. When he comes home from college, Jack's really lazy around the house.
6. Sam used to be a lot of fun, but now he's involved with some really dangerous people.

B *Over to you*

1. *In what circumstances would you* ***stand shoulder to shoulder*** *with someone?*
2. *In what circumstances would you* ***wash your hands*** *of someone?*

Now write

Write a paragraph about something that you would like to **try your hand** at some day. Explain why it interests you.

Unit 39

Feet and legs

not have a leg to stand on

drag your heels, *also* drag your feet

get off on the right foot

find your feet

jump in with both feet

land on your feet

your feet on the ground

pull someone's leg

dig your heels in

get off on the wrong foot

get your feet wet

kick up your heels

stand on your own (two) feet

put your best foot forward

put your foot down

Feet

- **dig your heels in,** *also* **dig in your heels** to refuse to change what you believe is right or what you want to happen
- **drag your heels,** *also* **drag your feet** to do something slowly because you do not want to do it
- **find your feet** to become familiar with a new place or situation
- **get off on the right foot** to begin doing something in a way that is likely to succeed
- **get off on the wrong foot** to begin doing something in a way that is likely to fail
- **get your feet wet** to experience something for the first time
- **jump in with both feet** to become involved in something quickly and completely
- **kick up your heels** to do things that you enjoy
- **land on your feet** to be in good or improved condition after a difficult experience
- **stand on your own (two) feet** to provide yourself with all the things that you need without asking for help
- **your feet on the ground** a realistic understanding of your own ideas, actions, and decisions
- **put your best foot forward** to act in a way that causes other people to have a good opinion of you
- **put your foot down** to tell someone that something must or must not happen

Legs

- **not have a leg to stand on** to have no support for your position
- **pull someone's leg** to tell someone something that is not true, as a way of joking with the person

Focus on meaning

Which definition?

Circle the best short definition for each idiom.

1. dig your heels in
   a. refuse to change
   b. be in good condition after a difficult time

2. drag your heels
   a. become familiar with something
   b. do something slowly

3. find your feet
   a. become familiar with something
   b. do something slowly

4. get off on the right foot
   a. start well
   b. do something quickly

5. get off on the wrong foot
   a. start badly
   b. do something slowly

6. get your feet wet
   a. experience something new
   b. become involved quickly, completely

7. jump in with both feet
   a. do something carefully
   b. become involved quickly, completely

8. kick up your heels
   a. refuse to change
   b. enjoy yourself

9. land on your feet
   a. try something new
   b. be in good condition after a difficult situation

10. not have a leg to stand on
    a. have no support for your position
    b. tell someone something that is not true

11. pull someone's leg
    a. have no support for your position
    b. tell someone something that is not true

12. put your best foot forward
    a. try something difficult for the first time
    b. act in a way that will cause people to think positively about you

13. put your foot down
    a. tell someone that something must (or must not) happen
    b. do something slowly

14. stand on your own two feet
    a. refuse to do something
    b. do things for yourself

15. your feet on the ground
    a. a realistic understanding of the situation
    b. in good condition after a difficult situation

Focus on form

A *Prepositions*

Use the prepositions in the box to complete the sentences. You will have to use one of the prepositions more than once.

down	forward	in	off	on	up

1. Even after he became famous, he still kept his feet ...on... the ground.
2. Try to put your best foot ....
3. Dad put his foot .... and said I'd have to get a job and

   stand .... my own two feet.
4. Go out, have fun, and kick .... your heels!
5. We were glad to see that they landed .... their feet.
6. He doesn't have a leg to stand ....
7. It's too bad they got .... the wrong foot.
8. Dig your heels .... and just say no.

B *Sentence completion*

Use these pairs of words to complete the sentences. You may have to change the form of some words.

find, feet	drag, heels	pull, leg	jump, both	get, wet	get, right

1. Why are you ...dragging... your ...heels...?
2. It took him time to .... his ....
3. I'm glad we .... off on the .... foot.
4. It's a good chance to .... your feet ....
5. He didn't think. He just .... in with .... feet.
6. Are you .... my ....?

Focus on use

A *What's your advice?*

You write an advice column in a newspaper. Read these letters. What is your advice to each of the writers? Use the idioms in the unit in your answers.

Ask *In the Know*

1. Dear *In the Know*:
We have just moved to a new city and we don't know anyone. There are lots of clubs we could join, but we're not sure we'd like the other people. What do you think we should do?

2. Dear *In the Know*:
I have an interview next week for a job overseas. I want to impress the firm, so I thought that I would dress in the national costume of the country I'd be working in. What do you think?

3. Dear *In the Know*:
My son is 26 years old. He has been living at home since he graduated from college four years ago. He has a good job and a nice girlfriend. My husband and I are retired. We would like to rent his room out. It would help pay the bills. What do you think we should do?

B *Over to you*

What are expressions in your language that mean the following?

1. *to do things you enjoy **(kick up your heels)***
2. *to take care of yourself **(stand on your own two feet)***
3. *to begin doing something in a way that is likely to succeed **(get off on the right foot)***
4. *to begin doing something in a way that is likely to fail **(get off on the wrong foot)***

Now write

Write a paragraph describing a time when you **pulled someone's leg** or someone pulled yours. What happened?

Unit 40

Water and waves

Water

- **blow something out of the water** to destroy something
- **blow you out of the water (1)** to completely surprise you
- **blow you out of the water (2)** to defeat or completely confuse you

*I can't understand this – camera manuals always **blow me out of the water.***

- **dead in the water** without any chance for success
- **in hot water** in a difficult situation in which you are likely to be punished
- **muddy the waters** to make a situation more confusing
- **not hold water** not to seem to be true or reasonable

- **test the waters** to check what people think about something before you start to use it
- **throw cold water on something** to criticize or stop something that some people are enthusiastic about
- **tread water** to be active without making progress or falling farther behind

*So far this year, we've just been **treading water**. We need to start increasing sales.*

- **water down something,** *also* **water something down** to make something weaker
- **water under the bridge** something that has happened and cannot be changed
- **between the devil and the deep blue sea** having only two very unpleasant choices

Waves

- **catch a/the wave** to understand and behave according to the most modern fashions in social behavior
- **make waves** to shock or upset people with something new or different
- **ride a/the wave of something** to be helped by being connected to something attractive or interesting

*He's been **riding the wave** of the family name for years.*

Focus on meaning

Key words

Put the idioms in the box under the key word that is the best match.

a. between the devil and the deep blue sea
b. blow something out of the water
c. blow you out of the water
d. catch the wave
e. dead in the water
f. in hot water
g. make waves
h. muddy the waters
i. not hold water
j. ride the wave of something
k. test the waters
l. throw cold water on something
m. tread water
n. water down something
o. water under the bridge

1. benefit from	2. difficult choice	3. confuse or surprise
d. catch the wave		

4. cause trouble	5. criticize	6. destroy/destroyed

7. experiment	8. in trouble	9. past

10. stay the same	11. not true or reasonable	12. weaken

Focus on form

A *Water or wave?*

*Complete these idioms by adding either **water**, **waters**, **wave**, or **waves**.*

1. water down something
2. .... under the bridge
3. blow something out of the ....
4. catch the ....
5. dead in the ....
6. in hot ....
7. make ....
8. muddy the ....
9. not hold ....
10. ride the .... of something
11. test the ....
12. tread ....

B *Prepositions*

Use the prepositions in the box to complete the sentences. You will need to use some of the prepositions more than once.

between	down	in	of	on	out	under

1. I don't want to be the one to throw cold water on this.
2. It needs to be watered .... before we can present it.
3. Forget it. It's all water .... the bridge.
4. That magician blew us .... the water with his tricks.
5. The plan is dead .... the water – there's no money for it.
6. Don't worry. We've been .... hot water before.
7. He's been riding the wave .... his father's success all his life.
8. We're .... the devil and the deep blue sea on this one.

Focus on use

A *What do you say?*

Using idioms from the unit, what could you say in these situations?

1. You don't think someone's idea is reasonable or true.
2. You think a friend of yours is going to get into trouble.
3. You want to say that something is past now and nothing can change it.
4. You think someone should try out a new idea.
5. You think someone is confusing things. You want the person to stop.
6. You want to tell a friend not to upset someone or something.

B *Over to you*

The idioms ***tread water, test the waters,*** *and* ***water something down*** *are each based on the literal meaning of the phrase. Think of these phrases in your own language – are there idioms that are the same or similar?*

Now write

Write a paragraph about a time when you were caught **between the devil and the deep blue sea** *or* you were **blown out of the water** by something or someone.

Negotiation role play

Unit 11

Student A

You live in Loon Lake. You and your neighbors are at a meeting with the company EcoGolf. You are the spokesperson. You have discussed the issues with your neighbors, and you know what they think.

You and your neighbors want the company to:

- employ as many local people as possible – at least 65 percent of the staff
- offer low membership fees to the townspeople
- put in environmentally acceptable road access and parking
- make the complex as environmentally friendly as possible
- put at least one local representative on the advisory team

Negotiation role play

Unit 11

Student B

You represent EcoGolf. You are meeting with the people who live in Loon Lake. This is a big project. The company wants to reach an agreement with the townspeople and start work as soon as possible. You can agree to:

- employ 50 percent local people on the staff
- low membership fees for townspeople during off-peak hours, on weekdays only
- put in environmentally acceptable road access and parking
- make the complex as environmentally friendly as possible
- have an independent advisory team

Reference

add fuel to the fire to make a situation worse than it already is • *Should the government warn the public of terrorist threats, or is it just adding fuel to the fire?* ➔UNIT 37

against your better judgment [slightly formal] not the best decision you believe you could make • *I wasn't surprised when Scott's business failed because I had lent him the money for it against my better judgment.* ➔UNIT 11

all along the whole time • *Do you think he's been cheating us all along?* ➔UNIT 15

all in a day's work unusual for other people to have to do but not unusual for you • *A fancy dinner with a Hollywood celebrity is all in a day's work for this reporter.* ➔UNIT 18

all work and no play (makes Jack a dull boy) it is not good to work all the time • *You need to get out and have fun – you know, all work and no play.* ➔UNIT 18

and how [especially spoken] I agree very strongly • *"That was a great game last night!" "And how!"* USAGE: usually used as a separate sentence, as in the example ➔UNIT 1

an arm and a leg a lot of money • *The tickets cost an arm and a leg!* USAGE: usually used with the verbs **cost**, **pay**, and **charge**. ➔UNIT 10

around the clock all day and all night without stopping • *One lane on the bridge is closed around the clock for the next three months.* ➔UNIT 15

as old as the hills ancient • *Some of these rituals are as old as the hills.* ➔UNIT 20

as something as they come as much of a particular characteristic as possible • *Eric is as competitive as they come and always trying to win.* ➔UNIT 12

at death's door dying or very ill • *He was at death's door when a liver became available for transplant.* ➔UNIT 7

at first blush when first learning or thinking about something • *At first blush, the house seemed perfect – then we found out we had no heat or water.* ➔UNIT 9

at first hand from seeing or experiencing directly • *For Carter, the visit was a chance to see at first hand the life and work of someone he admired.* ➔UNIT 38

at odds (with somebody/something) [slightly formal] in disagreement • *Such behavior is clearly at odds with what civilized society expects.* ➔UNIT 1

at peace with something/yourself feeling calm and relaxed about something or yourself • *She is at peace with herself these days.* ➔UNIT 12

at the helm (of something) [slightly formal] in control • *He resigned and left the company last July after two years at the helm.* ORIGIN: based on the literal meaning of **helm**, the handle or wheel that controls the direction in which a ship travels ➔UNIT 30

at the moment now • *At the moment I'm living with my parents.* USAGE: often used to suggest that the situation may change soon ➔UNIT 15

at your best showing your most positive characteristics • *It was kind of a bad day for me and I wasn't at my best.* ➔UNIT 12

bang for the buck, *also* **bang for your buck** value in exchange for money or effort • *This is a great little red wine that gives you plenty of bang for the buck.* USAGE: often used with **more**, **bigger**, and other adjectives ➔UNIT 34

bare your soul to express your secret thoughts and feelings • *I couldn't believe it. I had just met the woman and here she was, baring her soul!* ➔UNIT 5

be all smiles very happy • *My boss has been all smiles lately, but I keep wondering why!* ➔UNIT 5

be none the wiser, *also* **not be (any) the wiser** to fail to understand something • *Isabel must have explained her idea three times to me, but I'm afraid I'm none the wiser.* ➔UNIT 17

(be) wise to someone/something, *also* **get wise to someone/something** to know about and not be fooled by someone or something • *He called in sick every Monday, and the boss soon got wise to him.* USAGE: often used in the form **wise up**: *I finally wised up to their scheme.* ➔UNIT 28

be yourself to act in a manner that suits your personality • *Now she can be herself again and wear whatever she wants.* ➔UNIT 12

beat a dead horse to waste time trying to do something that will not succeed • *Do you think it's worth sending my manuscript to other publishers, or am I just beating a dead horse?* ➔UNIT 35

beat around the bush to avoid talking about what is important • *Quit beating around the bush and tell me what you really think about my idea.* →UNIT 2

beat someone up, *also* **beat up someone** to criticize someone strongly • *The candidates spent the time beating each other up instead of talking about how to improve the economy.* →UNIT 21

beat the bushes to search everywhere for someone or something • *We don't have to beat the bushes to get good photographs – they mostly come to us from photographers we know.* ORIGIN: based on the practice in hunting of having someone hit bushes with a stick in order to force birds hiding in them to fly up into the air to be shot →UNIT 23

(it) beats me *also* **what beats me** [especially spoken] I do not know or understand. • *It beats me how he managed to survive alone in the mountains for three weeks.* USAGE: often said in answer to a question: *"How should we explain all this?" "Beats me."* →UNIT 28

the beauty of something a quality that makes something good, easy, or of value • *The beauty of the Internet is its openness.* →UNIT 34

beef up something, *also* **beef something up** to make something stronger or more effective • *The city is beefing up police patrols, putting more cops on the street where they can be seen.* →UNIT 32

behind the times old-fashioned • *When it comes to women's rights, my grandfather is way behind the times.* →UNIT 20

below par not feeling as good as usual; = **not up to par** →UNIT 7

bend someone's ear to talk to someone for a long time • *She spent the day at a conference bending the ears of some high school teachers.* →UNIT 2

bend the rules to allow something to be done that is not usually allowed • *We don't usually let students take books home, but I'll bend the rules this time.* →UNIT 30

the best of both worlds the most enjoyable or attractive features of two different things • *I have the best of both worlds because I live in the country but I'm only an hour from the city.* →UNIT 26

the best thing since sliced bread wonderful • *My kids think their new puppy is the best thing since sliced bread.* →UNIT 26

bet the farm, *also* **bet the ranch** to risk everything you have because you are certain of something • *No matter how confident you are in the future, you should never bet the farm on one idea.* →UNIT 31

between a rock and a hard place having only two very unpleasant choices • *The manager is between a rock and a hard place – she can proceed without authority or see an area she has responsibility for fail.* →UNIT 11

between the devil and the deep blue sea having only two very unpleasant choices • *Employees are between the devil and the deep blue sea – they can accept the new retirement package or lose their jobs.* →UNIT 40

(just) between you and me without telling anyone else • *Between you and me, I think she made up the whole story about being robbed.* →UNIT 2

a bird's-eye view the appearance of something seen from above, or a general view of something • *The large painting offers a bird's-eye view that shows the layout of the ancient city.* →UNIT 35

bite the hand that feeds you to severely criticize the person or organization that helps you or pays you • *It's unwise to bite the hand that feeds you, but journalists need to tell the truth about the news business.* →UNIT 21

bite your tongue to stop yourself from speaking • *He was angry and wanted to say so, but he bit his tongue.* →UNIT 2

black and white a very clear choice that causes no confusion • *When you're flying a plane, it's black and white – you can't be wrong, you've got to be right.* ORIGIN: based on the clear difference between the colors →UNIT 36

black out to stop being conscious • *I blacked out right after the accident.* →UNIT 36

a blast from the past something that makes you suddenly remember an earlier time in your life • *Here's a blast from the past – the 1960s group the Mamas and the Papas were inducted into the Rock and Roll Hall of Fame this week.* →UNIT 20

blessed with something lucky to have a special quality or character • *He's been blessed with a cheerful disposition.* →UNIT 12

blood is thicker than water family relationships are stronger and more important than something else • *The employees want to support the strike, but they all have families to think of – and blood is thicker than water.* ➔UNIT 8

blow hot and cold to be enthusiastic one moment and not interested the next • *It's impossible to have a healthy relationship with someone who blows hot and cold all the time.* ➔UNIT 4

blow off steam to do or say something that helps you get rid of strong feelings or energy • *Linda says singing is a way for her to let off steam.* ➔UNIT 5

blow smoke to deceive others • *He wanted everyone to think that he had a lot of experience, but I think he was just blowing smoke.* ➔UNIT 37

blow something out of the water to destroy something • *The virus blew my computer out of the water.* ➔UNIT 40

blow the whistle (on someone/something) to show to the public dangerous conditions or illegal activities • *I knew my company was polluting the water, but I was afraid I would lose my job if I blew the whistle on it.* USAGE: usually something bad is shown in the hope of correcting it. ➔UNIT 22

blow up in your face to unexpectedly fail • *We don't want to create a situation that could blow up in our faces.* ➔UNIT 25

blow you out of the water **1** to completely surprise you • *Her singing blew me out of the water.* • **2** to defeat or completely confuse you • *Those directions blew us out of the water – we couldn't follow them at all.* ➔UNIT 40

a bolt from the blue suddenly and unexpectedly • *Quinn's announcement that he is quitting came like a bolt from the blue.* ➔UNIT 36

bone up on something to study or improve your understanding of something, especially for a test • *The test includes history, math, and languages, so I'll have to bone up on a lot of subjects.* ➔UNIT 9

born to do something to have the natural ability to do something • *This sweet-voiced artist was born to sing.* ➔UNIT 19

born with a silver spoon in your mouth to have opportunities and advantages because you were born into a rich family • *Andy's success was not due to hard work – he was born with a silver spoon in his mouth.* ➔UNIT 8

the bottom fell out (of something) something suddenly lost value • *When the bottom fell out of the real estate market, a lot of people lost a lot of money.* ➔UNIT 34

the bottom of the barrel the worst or the least able members of a group • *There were only 40 students in the new class, and I think the admissions office was getting to the bottom of the barrel.* USAGE: sometimes used in the form **scrape the bottom of the barrel** ➔UNIT 26

the bottom of the heap, *also* **the bottom of the pile** the lowest rank within the group • *Being near the bottom of the heap, the company has nowhere to go but up.* ➔UNIT 26

the bottom of the ladder the lowest rank • *Because she was just out of college, her job was at the bottom of the ladder.* ➔UNIT 18

break bread with someone [slightly formal] to eat • *There were several chances for politicians and celebrities to meet and break bread with each other.* ➔UNIT 3

break even to earn as much money as you spent • *We don't want to make a profit, but we need to break even.* ➔UNIT 10

break out something, *also* **break something out** to make food or drink available • *Break out the champagne and drink to the couple's health!* ➔UNIT 3

bring home the bacon to earn money to live on • *I stay home with the kids and Ann brings home the bacon.* ➔UNIT 10

bring it on to begin a fight or competition • *Bring it on – we're ready for you!* ➔UNIT 6

bring off something, *also* **bring something off** to succeed in doing something • *Only a megacorporation has the resources to bring off this kind of deal.* ➔UNIT 33

bring someone/something to mind, *also* **bring to mind someone/something** to cause you to think of someone or something • *That brings next month's meeting to mind.* USAGE: also used in the form **call to mind**: *He asked how I knew, and I couldn't call it to mind at the time.* ➔UNIT 29

brush up on something to study again something you learned before • *Brushing up on computer skills can be important for any worker thinking about getting a new job.* ➔UNIT 9

build bridges to increase understanding between different people or groups • *They hope an international conference will help to build bridges between their two countries.* ➔UNIT 14

burn your fingers to have a bad result from something, especially to lose money; = **get (your fingers) burned** ➔UNIT 37

burst into tears to suddenly cry • *Every time I think about his letter, I burst into tears.* ➔UNIT 5

by heart exactly and from memory • *You know the telephone number by heart, don't you?* USAGE: often used with **know**, **learn**, **recite**, and **play**: *My piano teacher wants me to learn the piece by heart.* ➔UNIT 29

call a spade a spade to tell the unpleasant truth about something • *Let's call a spade a spade – Brad is a very poor student.* ➔UNIT 27

call off the dogs, *also* **call off your dogs** to cause people to stop attacking or criticizing someone • *It's time to call off the dogs and let her get back to doing her job.* ➔UNIT 35

call the shots to make the important decisions • *The company was more successful when just one or two people were calling the shots.* ➔UNIT 30

carried away made very emotional or enthusiastic; = **swept away** ➔UNIT 4

carry off something, *also* **carry something off** to succeed in doing something • *She said she never lies because she doesn't have a good enough memory to carry it off.* ➔UNIT 33

carry the ball to do the work or take the responsibility necessary to achieve something • *The people who carried the ball for her campaign were mainly volunteers.* ➔UNIT 30

carry the day to win or succeed • *Senators in favor of cutting taxes carried the day.* ➔UNIT 33

(put) the cart before the horse to do something first that should happen only after something else has happened • *Barnhardt is putting the cart before the horse by building a stadium before a team has agreed to play here.* ➔UNIT 35

cast aspersions on someone/something to say that someone's character or work is bad • *When the exhibition of his paintings opened, some critics cast aspersions on both his art and his character.* ➔UNIT 21

catch the drift to understand in a general way what someone is telling you; = **get the drift** ➔UNIT 17

catch a / the wave to understand and behave according to the most modern fashions in social behavior • *The company's move was aimed at catching the wave of consumers rushing to the Web.* ORIGIN: based on the literal meaning of **ride a wave** (= to stand on a board moving across the rolling surface of the sea) ➔UNIT 40

a chip off the old block someone who is similar in character to his or her father or mother • *She's just like her mother – a real chip off the old block.* ➔UNIT 8

(have) a chip on your shoulder a tendency to get angry or upset easily • *He dropped out of high school and has had a chip on his shoulder ever since.* ➔UNIT 12

clam up to refuse to talk or answer • *Every time I think he's going to tell me what's bothering him, he just clams up.* ➔UNIT 2

a clean bill of health news that you are healthy or well • *He was given a clean bill of health by his doctor.* ➔UNIT 7

clean up to win or earn a lot of money • *We played poker last night, and I really cleaned up.* ➔UNIT 10

(as) clear as mud very difficult to understand • *His traffic directions were as clear as mud.* USAGE: used to humorously explain that there was a problem ➔UNIT 24

come across (as something) to appear to have a particular attitude or character • *He comes across as distant, but he's just shy.* ➔UNIT 12

come apart at the seams be in a bad condition and about to fail or lose control • *Large segments of the world economy seem to be coming apart at the seams.* ORIGIN: from the idea that when the **seams** (= places where two pieces of material are sewn together) in clothing come apart, it can no longer be used ➔UNIT 25

come clean to tell the truth about something you have tried to hide • *I should probably come clean now and admit that I really don't know how to cook at all.* ➔UNIT 27

come down with something to become ill with a particular disease • *I think I'm coming down with the flu.* ➔UNIT 7

come on strong to act in a forceful way • *I didn't want to come on too strong, so I tried not to seem angry.* ➔UNIT 32

come to blows to have a fight or serious argument • *Protestors nearly came to blows with police.* ➔UNIT 6

come to grips with something to make an effort to understand and deal with a problem or situation • *The whole community is struggling to come to grips with these kids' deaths.* ➔UNIT 17

come to light to become known • *Four soldiers have faced charges since the scandal came to light last fall.* ➔UNIT 23

come to the table to meet to discuss how to solve a problem or end a disagreement • *Carlson urged them to come to the table to resolve the issue.* ➔UNIT 11

come up with something to think of, develop, or find something • *They're trying to come up with a solution.* ➔UNIT 13

commit something to memory to study something in order to make yourself remember it • *Commit this number to memory.* ➔UNIT 29

compare notes to exchange information and opinions • *We met at the coffee shop to compare notes on our new boss.* ➔UNIT 2

connect the dots to understand the relationship between different ideas or experiences • *It took years of hard work to connect the dots between the murder and the suspect.* ORIGIN: from a children's activity in which a picture can be seen when you draw lines to connect numbered **dots** (= small round marks) ➔UNIT 17

cool down, *also* **cool off** to stop feeling angry • *I was really angry, so I left the house and took a walk to cool off.* ➔UNIT 4

crash and burn to fail suddenly and completely • *She watched her parents' marriage crash and burn.* ORIGIN: based on the image of a crash followed by a fire that completely destroys a vehicle or aircraft. ➔UNIT 25

the cream of the crop the best of a particular group • *This editorial staff isn't the cream of the crop, but it's not as bad as you say.* USAGE: based on the idea that cream is the best part of milk ➔UNIT 26

credit someone with something to believe that someone has a particular quality or ability • *I credited her with more sense than she showed.* ➔UNIT 19

dawn on you to suddenly understand something • *It finally dawned on him that she'd been joking and he was worried for no reason.* ➔UNIT 23

day and night all the time *It takes a while to get used to hearing traffic noise day and night.* ➔UNIT 15

dead in the water without any chance for success • *I guess our plans for a summer vacation are dead in the water.* ➔UNIT 40

dig in your heels, *also* **dig your heels in** to refuse to change what you believe is right or what you want to happen • *Be firm on important issues, but do not dig your heels in at every opportunity.* ➔UNIT 39

dirty your hands to involve yourself in doing work that is basic to something; = **get your hands dirty** ➔UNIT 18

dissolve into tears / laughter to lose control and express strong emotions • *She dissolved into tears when she saw the damage to her house.* ➔UNIT 5

do you a world of good to make someone feel much better • *Join the gym; it'll do you a world of good.* ➔UNIT 7

do the dirty work to do the unpleasant or difficult things • *Well, usually I do the dirty work and someone else gets the credit for getting it done.* ➔UNIT 18

do your homework to learn everything you need to know before doing something • *If you had done your homework, you would have known it was a silly question to ask.* ➔UNIT 9

down in the dumps unhappy • *She's down in the dumps because all of her friends are out of town.* ➔UNIT 4

down the line, *also* **down the road** [especially spoken] in the future • *Waiting even a year to put money into your retirement account can make a big difference down the line.* ➔UNIT 15

drag your heels, *also* **drag your feet** to do something slowly because you do not want to do it • *He knows he should make a decision, but he's dragging his feet.* ➔UNIT 39

draw fire to attract criticism • *The advertisements have drawn fire from parents' groups.* ➔UNIT 21

draw someone out, *also* **draw out someone** to persuade someone to express their thoughts and feelings • *She was good at drawing out young people and getting them to talk about their dreams.* ➔UNIT 2

draw the line at doing something to decide you will not do something • *I am a loyal employee, but I draw the line when I am asked to do something I think is wrong.* USAGE: often used to say you will not do something because you think it is wrong →UNIT 11

drill something into someone to have something repeated very frequently • *You learn vocabulary by having it drilled into you.* →UNIT 9

drink to someone to wish good health or good luck to someone • *Let's drink to Jessica's new job.* →UNIT 3

drive someone up the wall to make someone very unhappy and full of anxiety or anger • *Working on a computer all day drives me up the wall.* →UNIT 4

drop the ball to fail to keep working to reach a goal • *Public schools have pretty much dropped the ball on arts education.* ORIGIN: based on games like football in which all play stops if the ball is dropped →UNIT 25

drop-dead date a time by which something must be done • *He said the drop-dead date was December 31; after that no funds would be available.* →UNIT 15

drown your sorrows to drink a lot of alcohol because you want to stop feeling sad • *Frank insisted that I accompany him to his house, where I could drown my sorrows.* →UNIT 3

duck out (of somewhere) to leave a place quickly and without being noticed • *The press was waiting for us outside the hospital, so we ducked out a side door.* →UNIT 16

(as) easy as pie very easy • *You make everything sound as easy as pie, George.* USAGE: also used in the form **(as) easy as falling off a log** →UNIT 24

eat like a horse to eat large amounts of food often • *I eat like a horse, but I eat healthy food.* →UNIT 3

eat somebody out of house and home to eat a large amount of food in someone's home • *The boys have only been back two days, and they've already eaten me out of house and home.* →UNIT 3

every now and then sometimes • *We still meet for lunch every now and then, but not as often as we used to.* →UNIT 15

explode in your face to unexpectedly fail; = **blow up in your face** →UNIT 25

fair and square honestly • *We played very well and won, fair and square.* →UNIT 27

fall down on the job to fail to do something that you were expected to do • *Someone fell down on the job and didn't catch the obvious mistakes in the ad.* →UNIT 18

fall flat (on your face) to fail completely • *It used to be an amazing magazine, but it's fallen flat on its face.* →UNIT 25

fall in love (with someone) to begin to love someone • *The movie tells the story of a country doctor who falls in love with a beautiful waitress.* →UNIT 14

fall into someone's hands to be caught or controlled by someone • *There is a great concern that such dangerous weapons might fall into rebel hands.* USAGE: sometimes used in the form **fall into the wrong hands** →UNIT 38

fan the flames (of something) to make a bad situation worse • *These images of war could be used to fan the flames of hatred against our country.* ORIGIN: based on the literal meaning of **fan the flames** (= to cause air to flow toward a fire) →UNIT 37

farm out to give work or responsibilities to other people • *Magazines often farm out articles to freelance writers.* →UNIT 18

feel at home comfortable and relaxed • *They always make us feel at home when we visit them.* USAGE: sometimes used in the form **make yourself at home** →UNIT 8

a feel for something an understanding or ability in a particular subject or activity • *She has a real feel for language, so her books are a pleasure to read.* →UNIT 19

feel something in your bones to know something is true, although it cannot be proved • *I knew something terrible was going to happen – I could feel it in my bones.* →UNIT 28

feel your oats to have great confidence in your importance or ability • *Workers are feeling their oats and demanding higher wages.* →UNIT 19

your feet on the ground a realistic understanding of your own ideas, actions, and decisions • *It is hard to keep your feet on the ground when you suddenly become famous.* USAGE: sometimes used in the form **both feet on the ground** →UNIT 39

ferret out something, *also* **ferret something out** to discover something after careful searching • *If you're looking for owners of abandoned property, it can take years to ferret them out.* ➔UNIT 23

fight fire with fire to deal with someone in the way they are dealing with you • *In the face of stiff competition, we had to fight fire with fire and lower our prices.* ➔UNIT 37

fight for your life to try to stop a deadly illness or injury • *His brother was fighting for his life in a San Francisco hospital.* ➔UNIT 7

fight it out to argue fiercely until agreement is reached • *The boss decided to let the workers fight it out between themselves.* ➔UNIT 6

fight off something, *also* **fight something off** to try to end or prevent an illness • *Her body couldn't fight off the infection.* ➔UNIT 7

fill in (for someone) to do someone else's job temporarily • *He discovered his love of acting when he filled in for a sick friend in a college play.* ➔UNIT 18

find your feet to become familiar with a new place or situation • *New students need a little time to find their feet.* ➔UNIT 39

fish or cut bait to decide to act or do anything • *The time has come when you have to either fish or cut bait – either you help us plan what to do or we will decide and go ahead without you.* ➔UNIT 35

flex your / its muscles to use or increase your influence or power • *Conservatives are flexing their muscles in local elections this fall.* ➔UNIT 32

fly by the seat of your pants to do something difficult without the necessary experience or ability • *None of us had ever worked on a magazine before, so we were flying by the seat of our pants.* ➔UNIT 19

for the birds without value • *"What do you think of the new system?" "I think it's for the birds – it won't work."* ORIGIN: based on the idea that birds eat seed, which is not worth much ➔UNIT 35

for the long haul for a long period of time • *Before you invest in Internet stocks, be sure that you can afford to invest for the long haul.* USAGE: also used in the form **over the long haul** ➔UNIT 15

for the time being at this time • *This is probably as good a deal as we're going to get, at least for the time being.* ➔UNIT 15

from the bottom of your heart [especially spoken] with sincere feeling • *And I say from the bottom of my heart, I am so happy to be back in South Africa.* ➔UNIT 27

(straight) from the horse's mouth from someone who has the facts • *"Are you sure she's leaving?" "Definitely, I heard it straight from the horse's mouth."* ➔UNIT 35

from the sublime to the ridiculous from something that is very good to something that is very bad or silly • *The performances at the festival ranged from the sublime to the ridiculous.* ➔UNIT 26

full of yourself thinking that you are very important in a way that annoys other people • *He would be more fun to be around if he weren't so full of himself.* ➔UNIT 12

gales of laughter sudden loud, happy sounds made by people when they are amused • *I heard gales of laughter coming from the conference room.* ➔UNIT 5

get a fix on something, *also* **get a handle on something** to understand something • *It's not easy to get a fix on this new era we've entered.* ➔UNIT 17

get a grip (on yourself) to control your emotions • *Oh, get a grip! It's not as bad as you think!* ➔UNIT 5

get a second wind, *also* **get your/its second wind** to have increased energy or strength after feeling tired or weak • *The automobile industry seems to have gotten a second wind.* ➔UNIT 32

get away from it all to go somewhere that is completely different from what is usual • *You need to get away from it all for a while.* ➔UNIT 16

get back on your feet feeling better • *Phil will probably be back on his feet sooner than his doctor thinks he will.* ➔UNIT 7

get choked up to have difficulty speaking because you feel a great emotion • *During his farewell speech, the coach got all choked up and started to cry.* ➔UNIT 4

get off on the right foot to begin doing something in a way that is likely to succeed • *We like to start our meetings on time, and we got off on the right foot this morning.* ➔UNIT 39

get off on the wrong foot to begin doing something in a way that is likely to fail • *Holly's new secretary really got off on the wrong foot by being rude to visitors.* ➔UNIT 39

get off your high horse to stop acting as if you are better or more intelligent than other people • *He never got off his high horse long enough to consider how insulting his words were to many immigrants.* ➔UNIT 35

get over something to feel better after an illness or bad experience • *She's just getting over the flu.* ➔UNIT 7

get something off your chest to tell someone about something that has been worrying you • *Sometimes it's good to discuss your problems, just to get them off your chest.* ➔UNIT 5

get the drift to understand in a general way what someone is telling you • *I usually just read the first page of a report to get the drift.* ➔UNIT 17

get (the) first crack at something to have the first chance to try to do something; = **have (the) first crack at something** ➔UNIT 31

get the picture to understand a situation • *The team won two games, then lost two, then won two – you get the picture?* ➔UNIT 17

get through (to someone) to communicate with someone by telephone • *If you have trouble getting through, e-mail him.* ➔UNIT 2

get to the bottom of something to discover the truth about something • *The electric company has not yet gotten to the bottom of why we had such a huge blackout.* ➔UNIT 27

get up on the wrong side of (the) bed to begin the day feeling unhappy and uncomfortable • *I got up on the wrong side of the bed yesterday, and everything that could go wrong did.* ➔UNIT 4

get wind of something to learn about something secret • *As soon as we got wind of the concert, I ordered the tickets.* ➔UNIT 2

get your feet wet to experience something for the first time • *If you've never invested money in the stock market, now is the time to get your feet wet.* USAGE: said especially about something that involves taking a risk ➔UNIT 39

get (your fingers) burned to have a bad result from something, especially to lose money • *Many investors got burned on those stocks.* ➔UNIT 37

get your foot in the door to have an opportunity • *This part-time work has allowed Frank to get his foot in the door, and he hopes it will lead to a full-time job.* ➔UNIT 31

get your hands dirty to involve yourself in doing work that is basic to something • *She'll organize the event, but she doesn't like to get her hands dirty by selling tickets.* ➔UNIT 18

get your mind around something, *also* **get your head around something** to succeed in understanding something difficult or strange • *I still can't get my mind around the cruel things she said last night.* ➔UNIT 17

get your money's worth [especially spoken] to receive good value for the amount you have paid • *When I see how much I spend on repairs, I wonder if I got my money's worth with this car.* ➔UNITS 10, 34

get your own way to succeed in being allowed to do what you want • *He's enormously likable and charming and usually gets his own way.* ➔UNIT 30

getting on in years becoming old • *She's getting on in years, but she's healthy.* ➔UNIT 20

give and take the exchange of some of what you want for some of what someone else wants • *We reached an agreement after many hours of bargaining and give and take.* ➔UNIT 11

give someone/something the green light, *also* **give the green light to someone/something** to give permission for something to happen • *She's waiting for her doctor to give her the green light to play in Saturday's game.* USAGE: also used in the form **give a green light**: *The House of Representatives gave a green light to oil exploration off the East Coast.* ➔UNIT 36

give someone a hand, *also* **give a hand to someone** to help someone • *If you have any trouble with your homework, I'll be glad to give you a hand.* ➔UNIT 38

give someone a hard time to criticize or make life difficult for someone • *We were trying to help Tim, not just give him a hard time about his bad grades.* ➔UNIT 21

given half a chance allowed any opportunity • *Given half a chance, most writers would rather talk about a project than work on it.* USAGE: also used in the form **give someone/something half a chance** ➔UNIT 31

go after someone/something to attack or try to hurt someone or something • *The candidate went after his opponent in a very personal way.* ➔UNIT 21

go at someone, *also* **go at it** to attack or fight with someone • *The neighbors went at it until someone called the police.* →UNIT 6

go back a long way to know someone for a long time • *Justin and I go back a long way – we were in college together.* →UNIT 14

(go) back to the drawing board to start something again because the previous attempt failed • *Researchers went back to the drawing board to find where they went wrong.* USAGE: sometimes used without **go**: *I thought we were finished, then the boss sent us back to the drawing board.* →UNIT 25

go ballistic to become extremely upset and excited • *Chris went ballistic when they told him the plane was overbooked.* →UNIT 5

go belly up to fail • *My company announced layoffs, so I found another job and then my new company went belly up.* USAGE: usually said about business and other organizations →UNIT 25

go down in flames, *also* **go up in flames** to fail or end suddenly and completely • *We've seen two big mass transit plans go down in flames in recent years.* →UNIT 37

go down the tubes [especially spoken], *also* **go down the tube** to fail or become much worse • *His business is going down the tubes, and he's about to lose his house.* →UNIT 25

go figure I do not understand this • *The paint was really good, so they stopped making it – go figure, right?* →UNIT 17

go for broke to risk everything and try as hard as possible to achieve something • *You can't possibly go for broke if you're afraid of what might happen if you don't succeed.* →UNIT 31

go from bad to worse to become even more difficult or unpleasant • *The Tigers lost their first game 25 to 0, and then things went from bad to worse the following week when they lost by 38 points.* →UNIT 26

go hand in hand to be present together • *I thought ability in math and music were supposed to go hand in hand, but Tyler's much better in music than math.* →UNIT 38

go over someone's head **1.** to fail to understand something • *She was being sarcastic, but he took her seriously – the joke went totally over his head.* →UNIT 17 • **2.** to deal with someone at a higher level • *I would occasionally go over my manager's head to complain to the top financial officer.* →UNIT 18

go south to lose value or quality • *She decided to sell her stocks at the end of the year because she felt the market was going south.* →UNIT 34

go to the dogs to become worse in quality or character • *It is sad to report that this once first-class hotel has gone to the dogs.* →UNIT 35

go up in smoke to be wasted • *The research project was canceled and five years of hard work went up in smoke.* →UNIT 37

going around affecting a lot of people • *There's a virus going around.* →UNIT 7

(to have) got it bad to be very much in love • *I played the message again just to hear her voice and thought, boy, I've got it bad.* →UNIT 14

the greatest thing since sliced bread wonderful; = **the best thing since sliced bread** →UNIT 26

green with envy wishing very much that you had what someone else has • *Sharon's going off to the south of France for three weeks, and we're all green with envy.* →UNIT 36

hammer something out to create an agreement or solution to a problem • *After months of talking, we have begun to hammer out a deal that will join our two companies.* →UNIT 11

hand down something, *also* **hand something down** to give something old or used to a younger member of the family • *She treasures a watch her father handed down to her when she was a child.* →UNIT 8

(as) hard as nails strong and determined; = **(as) tough as nails** →UNIT 32

a hard nut (to crack) a difficult problem to solve; = **a tough nut (to crack)** →UNIT 13

someone/something has more bark than bite, *also* **someone's/something's bark is worse than his/her/its bite** something is not as unpleasant as you expected • *The storm turned out to have far more bark than bite.* • *My boss sounds tough, but her bark is worse than her bite.* →UNIT 35

have a good run, *also* **have a great run** to experience success • *Our industry is probably going to have a good run for the next several years.* →UNIT 33

have a hand in doing something to take part in an activity • *We don't put our label on anything unless we have a hand in designing and producing it.* →UNIT 38

have a head for something to have a natural ability to do something well • *I never had a head for music.* →UNIT 19

have a lump in your throat a strong feeling of emotion that makes speaking difficult • *He still couldn't watch the video without getting a lump in his throat.* →UNIT 4

have bags under your eyes to have dark circles under your eyes • *I can always recognize the new parents – they're the ones who have bags under their eyes.* →UNIT 7

have bigger fish to fry, *also* **have other fish to fry** to have something more important or more interesting to do • *I couldn't spend a lot of time on the problem – I had other fish to fry.* →UNIT 35

you have got to be kidding I am very surprised and cannot believe you are serious • *You want me to drive into the city in this rain? You've got to be kidding!* →UNIT 1

have it in you to possess a particular ability • *His speech was really funny – we didn't know he had it in him.* →UNIT 19

have it out (with someone) to argue or fight with someone because they have done something that made you angry • *Johnny had it out with Richie in the bar, and we all got thrown out in the end.* →UNIT 6

have one foot in the grave to be likely to die soon • *He had one foot in the grave when he volunteered to receive the world's first artificial heart.* →UNIT 7

have seen better days something is in bad condition because of heavy use • *The airport building had seen better days and needed a lot of repairs.* →UNIT 20

have something down pat to learn something so well that you do not have to think about how to do it or say it • *Bud had his answers down pat, but he knew there could be some questions on the test he hadn't thought of.* →UNIT 28

have something in common (with someone/something) to share interests or characteristics • *The two men had a lot in common and got along well.* →UNIT 14

have (the) first crack at something to have the first chance to try to do something • *If you want to sell your share of the business, our company would have first crack at buying it.* USAGE: sometimes used in the forms **get a crack at something** or **have a crack at something** →UNIT 31

have the last laugh to succeed when others thought you would not • *The company fired her last year, but she had the last laugh because she was hired by their main rival at twice the salary.* USAGE: sometimes used with **get**: *She said I'd never graduate, but I got the last laugh.* →UNIT 33

have your finger on the pulse (of something) knowledge of what is now happening in a particular area • *They've got their finger on the pulse of popular culture in Latvia.* →UNIT 28

have your foot in the door to have an opportunity; = **get your foot in the door** →UNIT 31

have your hands full to be very busy • *She has her hands full raising their eight children.* →UNIT 38

have your work cut out for you to have to do something you know will be difficult • *If that report is going to be finished by tomorrow, she has her work cut out for her.* →UNIT 18

head and shoulders above someone/something much better than other similar people or things • *Chicago's basketball team may be the oldest, but it is still head and shoulders above the rest of the league.* →UNIT 26

(be) head over heels (in love) to be in love with someone very much • *It's obvious that they're head over heels in love with each other.* →UNIT 14

your heart isn't in it you do not feel something is exciting or interesting enough to do • *I tried to do some writing, but my heart wasn't in it.* USAGE: sometimes used in the form **your heart isn't in something** →UNIT 4

(have a) heart of gold a kind and generous character • *He plays the part of a tough cop with a heart of gold.* →UNIT 12

a heart of stone an unfriendly and unkind character • *The sad condition of these refugees would move a heart of stone to sympathy.* →UNIT 12

hell on wheels extremely difficult • *He's going to be hell on wheels to deal with.* →UNIT 24

the here and now the present • *Jazz and hip-hop and the blues talk about the here and now in a way that everyone can understand.* →UNIT 15

hit a home run to succeed with something • *We felt our band hit a home run that night – it was the best performance we ever gave.* ORIGIN: based on the literal meaning of **home run** (= a play in baseball in which the person hitting the ball scores) →UNIT 33

hit a (raw) nerve to cause an emotional reaction; = **touch a (raw) nerve** →UNIT 4

hit a snag to experience a difficulty • *Our plans for Polly's surprise party hit a snag when we discovered she would be away that weekend.* →UNIT 13

hit it off (with someone) to be friendly with each other immediately • *We hit it off beautifully – we liked all the same things and we liked each other a lot.* →UNIT 14

hit pay dirt, *also* **strike pay dirt** to succeed • *He hit pay dirt with his next movie, which grossed $270 million worldwide.* ORIGIN: based on the literal meaning of **pay dirt** (= dirt that contains valuable metals) →UNIT 33

hit the deck, *also* **hit the dirt** to fall to the ground suddenly to avoid danger • *The kid next door threw a rock at him, but Ted hit the dirt and the rock didn't hit him.* →UNIT 22

hit the jackpot to succeed • *I think we hit the jackpot with our ad campaign because our sales nearly doubled.* ORIGIN: based on the meaning of **jackpot** (= a large amount of money you can win in a game) →UNIT 33

hit the road to begin traveling • *I'd love to stay longer, but it's time to hit the road.* →UNIT 16

hit the skids to fail • *His career really hit the skids after his divorce.* USAGE: often used in the form **on the skids** (= failing): *I can't believe that a whole industry is on the skids.* →UNIT 25

hold someone's feet to the fire to cause someone to feel pressure or stress • *I think reporters really should hold the president's feet to the fire about this issue.* →UNIT 37

hold your tongue to say nothing or to stop speaking • *He wanted to tell her the secret, but wisely decided to hold his tongue.* →UNIT 2

home away from home a place where you feel as comfortable as you do in your own home • *I stay in this hotel so often, it's become a home away from home for me.* →UNIT 8

horse around to be active in a silly way • *Stop horsing around and pay attention to your father!* →UNIT 35

hot and heavy full of very strong feelings • *The argument is still going hot and heavy about whether genetically modified foods are safe to eat.* →UNIT 6

a house of cards an organization or a plan that is very weak and can easily be destroyed • *Their partners began to suspect that the company was a financial house of cards.* ORIGIN: based on the literal meaning of **house of cards** (= a small structure made of playing cards) →UNIT 32

how's that? [especially spoken] I do not understand. • *"What time do you close?" "How's that?"* →UNIT 17

hung up on someone in love with someone in a foolish way • *Jeff's hung up on that actress he met at a party.* →UNIT 14

in a (New York) minute very quickly • *I would sell that car in a New York minute if the right offer came along.* →UNIT 15

in a bind forced to deal with a difficult situation • *Joe was in a bind, with two completely different sets of directions he was supposed to follow.* →UNIT 13

in a tight spot in a difficult situation • *If there is a shortage of fuel, everyone who drives to work will be in a tight spot.* →UNIT 13

in black and white **1** written or printed form • *Your offer sounds good, but I want you to put it in black and white.* →UNIT 36 • **2** as involving clear choices • *She tends to view the political world in black and white, with good guys and bad guys.* →UNIT 36

in dire straits in extreme danger or difficulty • *His family is in dire financial difficulty.* →UNIT 13

in hot water in a difficult situation in which you are likely to be punished • *Those e-mails complaining about your boss could land you in hot water.* →UNIT 40

in its own right because of your own ability or effort; = **in your own right** →UNIT 19

in jeopardy in danger • *It worries me that the money for these projects is in jeopardy, and I wonder what we will do if there is no money.* →UNIT 22

in the back of your mind, *also* **at the back of your mind** understood or known but not actively considered • *I'd like to believe we can still be friends, but in the back of my mind, I know that's not true.* →UNIT 29

in the black earning more money than you are spending • *Some states have legalized gambling as a way to put their finances in the black.* →UNIT 36

in the bosom of your family [slightly formal] in a safe or comfortable place, especially with family • *I often dreamed about being back in the bosom of my family.* →UNIT 8

in the doghouse in a situation in which someone is annoyed with you because of something you did • *The president's aide is in the doghouse over remarks he made to the press.* ORIGIN: based on the idea of being punished like a dog who is made to stay in a **doghouse** (= a shelter used by a dog), away from people →UNIT 35

in the driver's seat in control of a situation • *Huge consumer demand for electricity has put energy companies in the driver's seat.* →UNIT 30

in the fullness of time [slightly formal] after enough time passes • *Carol is sure everything will be ready in the fullness of time.* →UNIT 15

in the know having full information about something • *Among those in the know, Andy is considered a brilliant ad writer.* →UNIT 28

in the line of fire in a situation in which you may be severely criticized • *Maria was willing to place herself in the line of fire and accept the blame if the music festival failed.* →UNIT 21

in the long run, *also* **in the long term** finally • *Good management in the long run brought improved conditions for the workers.* →UNIT 15

in the loop having knowledge of and involvement in something • *The boss makes sure everyone in the office is in the loop.* →UNIT 2

in the money having a lot of money • *We won! We're in the money now!* →UNIT 10

in the pink (of something) very strong and operating well • *Our business is in the pink these days.* →UNIT 36

in the red spending more money than you are earning • *The phone company found itself about $1.8 billion in the red.* →UNIT 36

in the short run for a short period of time • *Gas prices may rise in the short run, but they should fall again by the end of the year.* →UNIT 15

in the short term in the near future • *In the short term, the tax will bring money into the treasury.* →UNIT 15

in touch (with someone) in communication with someone • *I'm sorry we haven't been in touch over the past few years.* USAGE: usually used with the verbs **be**, **keep**, **stay**, and **get** • Opposite **out of touch (with someone)** →UNIT 2

in your blood as a basic part of your qualities or characteristics • *She had the theater in her blood, and performing was as natural for her as breathing.* →UNIT 12

in your own right because of your own ability or effort • *This hospital is an extremely advanced critical care center in its own right.* →UNIT 19

something is anyone's guess, *also* **something is anybody's guess** no one knows the answer • *How the lawsuit will turn out is anyone's guess.* →UNIT 28

something is beyond me, *also* **it's beyond me** this is impossible to understand • *How they thought they could come in and out without anyone noticing is beyond me.* →UNIT 17

something is not a bed of roses something is not easy and without troubles • *He soon discovered that living in a foreign country is not always a bed of roses.* →UNIT 24

it doesn't take a rocket scientist to do something, *also* **you don't have to be a rocket scientist to do something** it is easy to understand or do something • *It doesn't take a rocket scientist to see that this school is in trouble.* USAGE: sometimes used in the form **it's not rocket science**: *A five-year-old could put this puzzle together – it's not rocket science.* →UNIT 24

(have) itchy feet to want to travel • *Winter's coming and I'm starting to get itchy feet.* →UNIT 16

jog your memory to cause you to remember something • *Maybe this picture will jog your memory.* →UNIT 29

jump all over someone, *also* **jump on someone** to criticize someone severely • *I know that some lawyers will jump all over me for agreeing with the prosecutors.* →UNIT 21

jump at the chance to quickly and eagerly accept an opportunity • *She jumped at the chance to go to Paris.* →UNIT 31

jump in with both feet to become involved in something quickly and completely • *When she decides to get involved, she jumps in with both feet.* →UNIT 39

keep a straight face to avoid showing any emotion, especially amusement • *It was hard to keep a straight face while I told him we weren't doing anything for his birthday.* →UNIT 5

keep abreast (of something) to have the most recent information about something • *This new service helps doctors keep abreast of the newest drugs available.* ➔UNIT 28

keep someone/something at arm's length to avoid becoming connected with someone or something • *Elizabeth makes me nervous, so I try to keep her at arm's length.* ➔UNIT 14

keep something in mind, *also* **keep in mind something** to remember a piece of information when you are doing something or thinking about a matter • *We will only have 20 minutes to argue our position – you must keep that in mind.* USAGE: also used in the form **bear something in mind** ➔UNIT 29

keep the peace [slightly formal] to prevent fighting or difficulties • *Troops were sent in to keep the peace in the region.* ➔UNIT 6

keep track of (someone/something) to continue to be informed or know about someone or something • *I've never been very good at keeping track of how I spend my money.* ➔UNIT 28

keep your hand in (something) to continue to be involved in something • *Rick turned the business over to his son, but he comes in Fridays to keep his hand in.* ➔UNIT 38

kick up your heels to do things that you enjoy • *In spring people dash outdoors to kick up their heels and join in their favorite sports.* ➔UNIT 39

knock off (something) to stop working for a time • *When do you knock off for the day?* ➔UNIT 18

knock something down to show that an idea or opinion is completely wrong • *Every time I make a suggestion, you knock it down.* ➔UNIT 21

know something inside out to be extremely well informed about something • *He knows New York inside out.* ➔UNIT 28

know something like the back of your hand to be very familiar with something • *He knows the nighttime sky like the back of his hand.* ORIGIN: based on the idea that you know what the back of your hand is like very well ➔UNIT 28

know your stuff to know a lot about a subject or be expert at doing something • *When it comes to fixing old cars, he really knows his stuff.* ➔UNIT 28

land on your feet to be in good or improved condition after a difficult experience • *It may take a few months to get a job, but I'm sure you'll land on your feet.* ➔UNIT 39

laughing all the way to the bank to be happy about the money earned by doing something • *The team's owners complain about the deal, but in fact they're laughing all the way to the bank.* ➔UNIT 10

lay down the law to tell people what they must do, without caring about their opinions • *I'm not going to let some new guy come into my office and start laying down the law.* ➔UNIT 30

lay it on the line to be completely honest • *The president laid it on the line today, stating economic sanctions would not be ruled out if negotiations stalled.* ➔UNIT 27

lay over to stop or have to stay in a place when you are traveling • *People were getting laid over in Dallas because of the floods in Houston.* ➔UNIT 16

lay someone/something open to something to put someone or something in a position where there is risk or danger • *The senator's remarks were thoughtless and laid him open to criticism.* ➔UNIT 22

lay your cards on the table to truthfully explain what you know or think; = **put (all) your cards on the table** ➔UNIT 11

learn something by rote automatically and without understanding • *The children had learned number facts by rote and could calculate quickly.* ➔UNIT 9

learn something the hard way to obtain knowledge or understanding through experience • *Since he won't take advice from anyone, I guess he is going to have to learn the hard way.* ➔UNIT 9

learn a/your lesson to understand something because of an unpleasant experience • *You hope that prisoners will say, "I don't want to end up back jail in again – I've learned my lesson."* ➔UNIT 9

learn the ropes to understand how to do a particular job or activity • *It'll take time for the new receptionist to learn the ropes.* ➔UNIT 9

leave no stone unturned to do everything possible in order to achieve or find something • *Both sides have vowed to leave no stone unturned in the search for peace.* ➔UNIT 23

leave the nest to move from your parents' home and live independently • *Our kids have all left the nest, and the house seems empty now.* ➔UNIT 8

leave you to your own devices to allow you to decide for yourself what you do • *Most of the time, the prisoners were left to their own devices by the guards.* ➔UNIT 30

lend a (helping) hand, *also* **lend someone a hand** to help do something • *Jay expected his children to lend a hand where they were needed.* ➔UNIT 38

lend an ear (to someone/something) to listen carefully and with understanding to someone • *She lent a sympathetic ear to my troubles.* ➔UNIT 2

let fly with something, *also* **let something fly** to express yourself in a way that will excite or anger others • *She turned and let fly with angry insults.* ➔UNIT 6

let off steam to do or say something that helps you get rid of strong feelings or energy; = **blow off steam** ➔UNIT 5

let someone have it to attack someone physically or with words • *When Joe got home late, Ann really let him have it.* ➔UNIT 6

let someone in on something to tell someone a secret • *The plan was so well guarded – they only let three people in on it.* ➔UNIT 2

let something slip through your fingers to waste an opportunity to achieve something • *This is my big chance to make a career in journalism, and I can't let it slip through my fingers.* ➔UNIT 31

let the cat out of the bag to tell something that is a secret, often without intending to • *Amazingly, not one of the people who knew about the surprise let the cat out of the bag.* ➔UNIT 35

light a fire under someone to make someone work harder or better • *It's time you lit a fire under those guys, or they'll never finish painting the house.* ➔UNIT 37

light up to look happy • *Her face lit up when she saw her old friends.* ➔UNIT 5

like pulling teeth extremely difficult • *Getting our kids dressed and off to school is like pulling teeth.* ➔UNIT 24

like taking candy from a baby extremely easy • *Selling my mother something I made is like taking candy from a baby – she can't say no.* ➔UNIT 24

live in the past to think or act as if conditions now are the same as long ago • *He believes the unions cannot live in the past and must deal with the changes in society.* ➔UNIT 20

long in the tooth to be very old • *Don't you think she's a bit long in the tooth to be a romantic heroine?* ➔UNIT 20

look a gift horse in the mouth to criticize or refuse to take something that has been offered to you • *I know the car's not in great condition, but you shouldn't look a gift horse in the mouth.* USAGE: based on the idea that you can discover a lot about a horse's condition by looking at its teeth ➔UNIT 21

look down on someone/something, *also* **look down your nose at someone/something** to consider someone or something as not important or of value • *"A lot of people look down on us because we're homeless," she says.* ➔UNIT 34

lose the thread (of something) to not be able to understand something that someone is saying because you are not giving it all your attention • *Jeb wasn't listening at all and lost the thread of what his father was saying.* ➔UNIT 17

lose track of someone/something to no longer be informed or know about someone or something • *I've lost track of most of my college friends.* • Opposite **keep track (of someone/something)** ➔UNIT 29

lose your head to lose control of your emotions • *I was so frightened, I completely lost my head.* ➔UNIT 5

lose your heart to someone/something to fall in love • *When she was 23 she lost her heart to a much older man.* ➔UNIT 14

lose your temper become very angry • *I lost my temper with him when his cell phone rang during class.* ➔UNIT 5

love at first sight an immediate, strong attraction for someone you just met • *She took an immediate liking to him – it was love at first sight.* ➔UNIT 14

lower your guard, *also* **drop your guard** to stop being careful of expressing your ideas or emotions • *When he found out I wasn't a journalist, he dropped his guard.* ➔UNIT 5

make a go of something, *also* **make a go of it** to try to succeed in an activity • *To make a go of it overseas, you have to respect the local culture and traditions.* ➔UNIT 33

make a killing to quickly earn a lot of money • *Ice cream trucks made a killing in the hot weather.* ➔UNIT 10

make a mental note to make an effort to remember something • *I made a mental note to call the dentist tomorrow.* ➔UNIT 29

make a mockery of something to make something seem stupid or without value • *The film makes a mockery of a serious illness.* ➔UNIT 34

make fun of someone/something to make someone or something seem foolish by making jokes about them • *When she first moved north, people made fun of her southern accent.* ➔UNIT 21

make good to become successful • *He was represented as the local boy who made good in Hollywood.* ➔UNIT 33

make heads or tails (out) of something to understand something • *The way the document was worded was incredibly complicated – no one could make heads or tails out of it.* USAGE: usually used in the negative ➔UNIT 17

make no bones about something to say clearly what you think or feel about something • *He made no bones about how bad he thought the food was.* ➔UNIT 27

make up for lost time to do as much as possible that you were not able to do before • *Ms. Wesley published her first novel when she was seventy and quickly made up for lost time by writing nine more.* ➔UNIT 15

make waves to shock or upset people with something new or different • *Her clothes have made waves on the fashion scene around the world.* USAGE: often used in the form **not make waves**: *We decided not to make waves and had a real wedding.* ➔UNIT 40

make your mouth water to feel pleasure at the thought of something particularly beautiful or good • *Such beauty is enough to make anyone's mouth water.* ORIGIN: based on the literal meaning of **make your mouth water** (= to cause your mouth to produce liquid when you see or think about food) ➔UNIT 26

make your presence felt to have a strong effect on other people or on a situation • *Hockney made his presence felt in the New York art world shortly after he arrived there.* ➔UNIT 32

a man (or person) of few words a man who speaks only when necessary • *He was respected as a man of few words and significant actions.* ➔UNIT 12

meet someone halfway to do some of what someone asks you to do • *He's put forward some good proposals for settling the strike, but the other side has not been willing to meet him halfway.* USAGE: often said about an attempt to reach agreement ➔UNIT 11

mend (your) fences to repair a relationship with someone • *The mayor is trying to mend fences with members of the city council so they will approve his plan.* ➔UNIT 14

your mind goes blank you cannot think of anything to say • *The teacher asked me a question, and my mind went blank.* ➔UNIT 29

a mind of your own the ability to act or think independently • *I advised her to take the job offer, but she has a mind of her own, so I don't know what she'll decide.* ➔UNIT 19

mind over matter thought is stronger than physical things • *Curing cancer may not be a question of mind over matter, but your attitude is important.* ➔UNIT 32

mind the store to be responsible for the operation of a business or organization • *The governor was on vacation then, and he was clearly not minding the store.* ➔UNIT 30

miss the boat to lose an opportunity that could lead to success • *He thinks we're missing the boat on improving relations with Russia.* ➔UNIT 31

miss the point to fail to understand what is important about something • *In case anyone missed the point of its weapons tests, the military practiced an island invasion the next month.* ➔UNIT 17

money is no object the cost of something is not important • *Where would you go on vacation if money were no object?* ➔UNIT 10

money talks money can influence what is done or how it is done • *They told him they didn't want to sell the house on the beach, but he said, "You'll sell – money talks."* ➔UNIT 10

muddy the waters to make a situation more confusing • *He's just trying to muddy the waters so we won't notice all the bad things he's done.* ➔UNIT 40

you must be kidding I am very surprised and cannot believe you are serious; = **you have got to be kidding** ➔UNIT 1

your nearest and dearest your family • *We don't get back to see our nearest and dearest very often.* ➔UNIT 8

a needle in a haystack something extremely hard to find • *It's pretty much a needle in a haystack because these fish are extremely hard to find.* USAGE: often used in the forms **look for a needle in a haystack** and **find a needle in a haystack** ORIGIN: based on the idea that it is almost impossible to find a thin sewing needle in a haystack (= a very tall pile of dried grass) ➔UNIT 23

night and day all the time; = **day and night** ➔UNIT 15

a nose for something a special ability to find or do something • *Any good journalist has a nose for a good story.* ➔UNIT 19

nose around to try to discover information • *Justice Department lawyers started nosing around after they received a complaint from a former employee.* ➔UNIT 23

not agree with you to make you feel sick • *Seafood just doesn't agree with me.* ➔UNIT 7

not all it's cracked up to be, *also* **not what it's cracked up to be** not as good or as special as people believed • *The general opinion is that love affairs aren't all they're cracked up to be.* ➔UNIT 26

not have a clue, *also* **without a clue** to have no knowledge or information about something • *The guy doesn't have a clue what forestry is all about.* USAGE: sometimes used in the form **have a clue**: *Before most doctors have a clue what a new drug can do, it's being sold to the public.* ➔UNIT 28

not have a leg to stand on to have no support for your position • *The company settled the lawsuit because they did not have a leg to stand on.* ➔UNIT 39

not have a type of bone in your body to have none of the characteristic described • *He was friendly and kind and didn't have a mean bone in his body.* ➔UNIT 12

not have the faintest idea, *also* **not have the foggiest idea** to not know anything at all about something • *I didn't have the faintest idea where I was or which way I was going.* ➔UNIT 28

not hold water to not seem to be true or reasonable • *That argument isn't likely to hold water with my father.* ➔UNIT 40

not know beans about something to know nothing about something • *I don't know beans about computers.* ➔UNIT 28

not up to par not feeling as good as usual • *He had to cancel the meeting because he wasn't feeling up to par.* ➔UNIT 7

not worth the paper something is printed on to have no value or importance • *He's got a degree from an online university that's not worth the paper it's printed on.* ➔UNIT 34

nothing to write home about not something that was especially good or exciting • *The food was all right but nothing to write home about.* USAGE: often used as a humorous way to describe something that is obviously bad: *War is nothing to write home about.* ➔UNIT 26

of a certain age not young • *Adults of a certain age might want to spend a couple of hundred dollars more for a larger monitor that will be much easier on their eyes.* USAGE: used to avoid saying **middle aged** or **old** ➔UNIT 20

off the beaten track not known by or popular with many people • *We try to find places off the beaten track where tourists don't usually go.* ➔UNIT 16

off the hook having avoided a difficult situation • *He's just happy to be off the hook on that harassment charge* USAGE: often used with **get** or **let**: She got him off the hook by lending him her class notes. ➔UNIT 30

on edge nervous or worried • *You're always on edge waiting for an important call because you don't know when the phone will ring.* ➔UNIT 4

on its last legs about to stop working. • *We've had the same vacuum cleaner for twenty years now, and it's on its last legs.* ➔UNIT 20

on someone's shoulders as a personal responsibility for someone • *A district attorney has an awful burden on his shoulders.* ➔UNIT 30

on the contrary just the opposite, especially of something said or believed • *The evidence of history, on the contrary, shows that these ancient people had a very advanced culture.* USAGE: often used to disagree with someone or something and to present new information ➔UNIT 1

on the fence not able to decide something • *Many consumers are still on the fence, waiting to see if a better, less expensive computer will come along.* USAGE: often used with **sit** ➔UNIT 11

on the go while traveling • *Cell phones are a simple and efficient way to send and receive e-mail on the go from almost anywhere.* ➔UNIT 16

on the job while working • *He's is always checking his workers to be sure they're wearing hard-hats on the job.* ➔UNIT 18

on the level honest or true • *We are there when the inspections are done, so we know that everything is on the level.* ➔UNIT 27

on the loose free to move about and dangerous • *Police warned that a serial killer is on the loose in the northwest.* ➔UNIT 22

on the mend getting better after an illness or injury • *I hurt my shoulder last month, but it seems to be on the mend.* ➔UNIT 7

on the road traveling to different places • *The band spends three months a year on the road.* ➔UNIT 16

on the rocks likely to fail because of serious problems • *It became clear that her 15-year marriage to David was on the rocks.* ➔UNIT 14

on the same wavelength, *also* **on the same page** in agreement • *Writing the screenplay was easy because Bill and I were on the same wavelength.* ➔UNIT 1

on the tip of your tongue about to be said • *Her name is right on the tip of my tongue.* ➔UNIT 29

on the up and up honest or legal • *There is no way to be sure that a salesman is on the up and up.* ➔UNIT 27

on the firing line, *also* **in the firing line** in a situation that attracts criticism • *The judge found himself on the firing line from women for remarks he made about discrimination in the workplace.* ➔UNIT 21

on your guard to be careful and aware because a situation might be dangerous • *I resent this attitude that you can't trust anybody, that you always have to be on your guard.* ➔UNIT 22

once in a blue moon [especially spoken] almost never • *Once in a blue moon we'll go out to dinner but we usually prefer to eat at home.* ➔UNIT 15

open up to talk in a free and honest way • *I felt I couldn't open up to anybody, not even to my best friend.* ➔UNIT 2

open season (on someone/something) a situation in which someone or something is criticized or treated unfairly • *She feels it's almost like someone has declared open season on anyone who looks like a foreigner.* ORIGIN: based on the literal meaning of **open season** (= the time of the year when hunting is legal) ➔UNIT 21

(be) out of luck not having an opportunity or situation that you want • *This type of racing bike only comes in large sizes, so if you're a short person, you're out of luck.* ➔UNIT 31

out of sorts in an unhappy mood • *He was feeling a little tired and out of sorts.* ➔UNIT 4

out of the blue, *also* **out of a clear blue sky** happening suddenly and unexpectedly • *Then, one day, completely out of the blue, I had a letter from her.* ➔UNIT 36

out of the frying pan (into the fire) from a bad situation to an even worse one • *Many kids who run away from unhappy homes discover they've jumped out of the frying pan into the fire when they try to live on their own.* USAGE: often used with **jump**, as in the example ➔UNIT 37

(be) out of your depth knowing very little about a subject • *I know I'm out of my depth with teenagers.* ➔UNIT 28

over the hill no longer able to do something at an acceptable level because of age • *Some judges who are 75 may be over the hill, but others still have energy galore.* ➔UNIT 20

over the moon extremely pleased and happy • *When he sent me flowers and a note, I was over the moon.* ➔UNIT 4

paint the town red to go out and celebrate without control • *John finished his exams today, so he's gone out to paint the town red.* ➔UNIT 36

paper over something, *also* **paper something over** to solve a problem temporarily • *They papered over their disagreements in order to end the meeting on a positive note.* ➔UNIT 13

part company (with someone) to end a relationship • *Rick and I parted company a long time ago, and I'm seeing someone else now.* ➔UNIT 14

pass up something, *also* **pass something up** to fail to take advantage of an opportunity • *When they invited her to perform, I told her she shouldn't pass it up.* ➔UNIT 31

past your/its prime no longer able to do something at an acceptable level because of age • *The dancer was past her prime, though she performed occasionally as a guest artist.* →UNIT 20

the path of least resistance the way that is the easiest • *Thieves usually take the path of least resistance, taking the cars that are easiest to steal.* →UNIT 24

a piece of cake something very easy • *Most parents know that dealing with a sick child makes everything else look like a piece of cake.* →UNIT 24

pick a fight (with someone), *also* **pick fights (with someone)** to intentionally start a fight or argument with someone • *She foolishly picked a fight with someone very powerful.* →UNIT 6

pick at food to eat food in small pieces and without enjoyment • *He eats very little, picking at his food with his fork.* →UNIT 3

pick up on something [especially spoken] to continue talking about something previously said • *I'd like to pick up on what Hayley was saying.* →UNIT 2

pick up something, *also* **pick something up** to learn something • *I was born up north, but I moved at such a young age that I picked up the southern ways quickly.* →UNIT 9

pick up speed to increase in value or degree • *Stocks picked up speed in the final hour of trading this afternoon.* →UNIT 34

pick you up to make you happy • *Seeing her always picked me up.* →UNIT 4

pig out to eat a lot • *Our kids dream of staying up late and pigging out on junk food.* →UNIT 3

a pillar of strength someone who is emotionally very strong • *Roger was a pillar of strength when my father died.* →UNIT 32

(as) plain as day easy to see or understand • *The secret to our success is as plain as day – make a good plan and stick to it.* →UNIT 24

play it safe to avoid any risk • *I like to play it safe with my investments.* →UNIT 31

play Russian roulette to take foolish and dangerous risks • *She accused the hospital of playing Russian roulette with the health of poor children.* ORIGIN: based on the literal meaning of **Russian roulette**: (= a dangerous game of chance in which you hold a gun containing one bullet to your head and shoot, winning if the bullet does not come out) →UNIT 22

play with fire do something that could cause you trouble later • *Don't you know you're playing with fire when you get involved with someone who's already married?* →UNIT 37

poke fun at someone/something to make someone or something seem foolish by making jokes about them; = **make fun of someone/something** →UNIT 21

poke your nose into something to try to discover things that do not involve you • *The government has no business poking its nose into people's personal lives.* →UNIT 23

the pot calling the kettle black a situation in which one person criticizes another for a fault they have themselves • *Ernie accused me of being selfish. Talk about the pot calling the kettle black!* →UNIT 36

pride yourself on something to value a special ability that you have • *He prides himself on his teaching.* →UNIT 19

prove your mettle, *also* **show your mettle** [slightly formal] to show that you are brave and have a strong character • *As a reporter, she certainly proved her mettle working in the midst of a war zone.* →UNIT 32

psych out someone, *also* **psych someone out** to make someone believe that they will fail • *Our strategy is to psych out the other team before the game begins.* →UNIT 25

pull down (an amount of money) to earn a lot of money • *He's just out of college and already pulling down $100,000 a year.* →UNIT 10

pull no punches to deal with something honestly without hiding anything • *The 20-minute training video pulls no punches – it is completely realistic.* USAGE: often used in the form **not pull any punches**: *The television network isn't pulling any punches with the subject matter on its new show.* →UNIT 27

pull off something, *also* **pull something off** to succeed in doing something difficult or unexpected • *I don't know how you pulled it off, but we're $5,000 richer today than we were yesterday.* →UNIT 33

pull someone's leg to tell someone something that is not true as a way of joking with them • *Is he really angry with me, or do you think he's just pulling my leg?* →UNIT 39

pull up roots to move away from a place where you have lived for a long time • *It's hard to pull up roots after living in the area for a long time.* →UNIT 8

pull your/its punches to deal with something in a way that is not completely honest • *I want you to tell me what you think – and don't pull your punches.* →UNIT 27

put (all) your cards on the table to truthfully explain what you know or think • *I can only put my cards on the table and say that we want this deal to work.* →UNIT 11

put all your eggs in one basket to risk something in support of one idea or plan • *I didn't want to put all my eggs in one basket, so I played five different lottery games.* ORIGIN: based on the idea that if all the eggs you got from your chickens are in one **basket** (= container) and you drop it, you will lose all your eggs. →UNIT 31

put away food or drinks to eat or drink a lot of something • *He put away a whole apple pie in one sitting.* →UNIT 3

put down roots to start to live in a place and feel that you belong there • *We knew this was where we wanted to put down roots the moment we arrived.* →UNIT 8

put (someone) out to pasture to make someone stop working at their job because they are too old to be useful • *At 62, he felt that he was not ready to be put out to pasture.* ORIGIN: based on the tradition of keeping farm animals that are too old to work in a **pasture** (= land covered with grass) →UNIT 20

put someone/something through his/her/its paces to test the ability or skill of a person or system • *Frank took the car for a drive through the mountains and really put it through its paces.* →UNIT 19

put someone's feet to the fire to cause someone to feel pressure or stress; = **hold someone's feet to the fire** →UNIT 37

put two and two together to understand something by using the information you have • *I didn't tell her George had left, but she noticed his car was gone and put two and two together.* →UNIT 17

put your best foot forward to act in a way that causes other people to have a good opinion of you • *All I could do was put my best foot forward and hope I made a good impression.* →UNIT 39

put your foot down to make a decision and firmly act on it • *Mom put her foot down and said I couldn't use the car until my grades improved.* →UNIT 39

put your heads together to share ideas in trying to solve a problem • *If we can put our heads together, we can figure out a way to deal with this.* →UNIT 13

put your life on the line to risk dying • *Politicians aren't putting their lives on the line to fight this war, but ordinary people must do that.* →UNITS 22, 31

put your two cents in to give your opinion • *She believes it is her duty to vote and put her two cents in.* →UNIT 1

puzzle out something, *also* **puzzle something out** to study something in order to understand it • *The reader shouldn't have to puzzle out what the writer means.* →UNIT 13

puzzle over something to give a lot of thought and attention to something • *I've been puzzling over it all week, but I haven't thought of a way out.* →UNIT 13

rack your brain to try very hard to remember or think of something • *I've been racking my brain trying to think of his e-mail address.* →UNIT 29

read between the lines to find a hidden meaning in something said or written • *The report doesn't criticize the research directly, but you can read between the lines that the committee wasn't impressed.* USAGE: sometimes used without the verb: *Leo read Melodie's letter again, hoping for some hidden message between the lines.* →UNIT 23

read up on something to learn a lot about something by reading a lot • *I've been reading up on Maine's history.* →UNIT 9

refresh your memory to help you remember something • *He refreshed his memory by rereading the notes taken at the meeting.* USAGE: often used by lawyers when asking questions in a trial: *"Will this photograph refresh your memory?"* →UNIT 29

reinvent the wheel to discover how to do something that has already been discovered • *We've had a lot of experience with disasters and don't have to reinvent the wheel every time something happens.* →UNIT 23

ride a wave of something, *also* **ride the wave of something** to be helped by being connected to something attractive or interesting • *The president rode a wave of good feeling among voters that made it impossible for him to lose the election.* ORIGIN: based on the literal meaning of **ride a wave** (= to stand on a board moving across the rolling surface of the sea) →UNIT 40

ring a bell to seem familiar • *Your name rings a bell. What company do you work for?* →UNIT 29

ring hollow, *also* **ring false** to seem dishonest, not true, or wrong • *The Rockets sounded like a defeated team – they talked of the possibility of a comeback, but the words rang hollow.* USAGE: often used in the forms **a hollow ring** or **a false ring** (= a dishonest or not sincere quality): *Her story about the hostages is certainly exciting, but it has a hollow ring.* →UNIT 27

ring true to seem accurate or sincere • *The book rang true because the author had actually experienced the ordeal of being marooned on an island.* USAGE: often used with **not**, as in the example, and often used in the forms **the ring of truth** or a **ring of truth**: *Speaking as a parent of boys, I can tell you her comments have the ring of truth.* →UNIT 27

risk your neck to do something dangerous • *We risked our necks to rescue you, and all you can say is "Gee whiz"?* →UNIT 22

roll out the red carpet (for someone) to give a special welcome to someone important • *This city has rolled out the red carpet for women's fashion buyers and the media.* ORIGIN: based on the literal meaning of **red carpet** (= a thick red covering for a floor that is put down for important guests to walk on) →UNIT 36

roll up your sleeves to prepare for hard work • *After the election, the mayor rolled up his sleeves and began immediately to put his promises into action.* →UNIT 18

run a fever, *also* **run a temperature** to have a high body temperature caused by illness • *She developed a bad ear infection and has been running a fever for two days.* →UNIT 7

run in the family, *also* **run in someone's family** to be a common quality among members of a particular family • *His father and uncle are good at sports – athletic ability seems to run in the family.* →UNIT 8

run rings around someone/something to show much more skill or ability than someone or something else • *International gangs of art thieves have run rings around national police.* →UNIT 19

a running battle (with someone/something) an argument or a fight that continues for a long time • *They have been fighting a running battle with their neighbors for years.* →UNIT 6

sail through something to easily succeed in something • *The voting machines sailed through their first election day test last Tuesday.* ORIGIN: based on the idea of a boat sailing smoothly on the water →UNIT 33

salt of the earth the best people, especially good, ordinary people • *Helen and Terry are good, decent people – the salt of the earth.* →UNIT 12

save the day to do something that solves a serious problem • *The hero saved the day by rescuing the hostages just in the nick of time.* →UNIT 13

say your piece to express your opinion about something, esp. something you do not like • *When the young man interrupted, the president stopped talking and let the man say his piece.* →UNIT 1

scrape by to come very close to failing • *She only scraped by in the last election and nobody expects her to win this time.* →UNIT 33

seal someone's/something's fate [slightly formal] to decide the future of someone or something • *The election of Abraham Lincoln sealed the fate of slavery.* USAGE: usually refers to an unsuccessful or unpleasant future →UNIT 11

see eye to eye to agree with someone • *My father and I see eye to eye on most things.* USAGE: often used in the form **not see eye to eye**: *We don't see eye to eye on a lot of things.* →UNIT 1

see red to become very angry • *Some Internet customers are seeing red as a result of the new virus that slowed down Web traffic last week.* →UNIT 36

see someone off, *also* **see off someone** to go with someone to the place where they will begin a trip • *My parents saw me off at the airport.* →UNIT 16

set off, *also* **set out** to start going somewhere • *He got a Guggenheim fellowship and set off for Mexico to write a novel.* →UNIT 16

set the record straight to tell the true facts that have not been accurately reported • *If we are wrong and Brian would like to set the record straight, he should come and talk to us.* →UNIT 27

set the world on fire to be very exciting or successful • *The new video game format set the world on fire with huge sales at Christmas.* →UNIT 37

settle down to accept responsibilities and behave in a more regular way than you have in the past • *It's time you settled down.* →UNIT 8

settle in to begin to feel comfortable in a new place • *Have you settled in to your new home yet?* →UNIT 8

several irons in the fire a number of jobs or possibilities available at the same time • *Job counselors recommend keeping several irons in the fire when you're looking for work.* →UNIT 37

a shadow of your/its former self a smaller, weaker, or less important form of someone or something • *With most of its best players traded away, the team was reduced to a shadow of its former self.* →UNIT 32

a shot in the arm a strong positive influence • *Winning this award is a big shot in the arm for our students.* →UNIT 32

a shoulder to cry on someone who gives you sympathy when you are upset • *My father had just died, and I needed a shoulder to cry on.* →UNIT 38

show someone the door to make someone leave • *Dick was rude to my family, so I showed him the door.* →UNIT 16

show your hand to let others know what you are planning to do; = **tip your hand** →UNIT 11

a sight for sore eyes something you are happy to see • *A taxi is a sight for sore eyes when it's raining.* →UNIT 4

slip out to leave quickly and quietly • *I'll try to slip out at lunchtime and see if I can find her.* →UNIT 16

slip your mind to be forgotten • *With all this going on, the concert completely slipped my mind.* →UNIT 29

slow on the uptake not able to understand something quickly • *I tried to explain how the new software works to my manager, but he's a little slow on the uptake.* →UNIT 17

smoke and mirrors something that is meant to confuse or deceive people • *Is this crisis just so much smoke and mirrors, or is it true that the government will run out of money?* →UNIT 37

smoke someone out to force someone to stop hiding • *To prevent such attacks you have to smoke out the bad guys before they reach their targets.* →UNIT 37

sniff out someone/something, *also* **sniff someone/something out** to discover someone or something, usually only after a special effort • *Part of their job is to sniff out talented new writers.* →UNIT 23

soak up something, *also* **soak something up** to learn and remember something quickly and easily • *Jill soaks up everything that's said in class.* →UNIT 9

something comes back (to someone) to remember something • *Wait! It came back to me – her name is Lyn.* →UNIT 29

sound someone out, *also* **sound out someone** to carefully discover what someone thinks or knows • *I thought it might be good to sound him out about having you come to work for us.* USAGE: used to describe a way of asking about someone's opinions without upsetting or angering them →UNIT 1

speak up to express your opinion • *If you need help, you have to speak up or no one will know.* →UNIT 1

split the difference to accept only part of what was originally wanted • *When they don't agree, she's always trying to get them to split the difference so everyone will be happy.* →UNIT 11

spoiling for a fight to be very eager to fight or argue • *He says what he thinks, and so people think he's always spoiling for a fight.* →UNIT 6

stand on your own (two) feet to provide yourself with all the things that you need without asking for help • *It's time that kid learned to stand on his own two feet.* →UNIT 39

stand out like a sore thumb to be easily noticed and different; = **stick out like a sore thumb** →UNIT 38

stand shoulder to shoulder to support one another during a difficult time • *The whole town stood shoulder to shoulder while the rescue workers struggled to free the trapped miners.* →UNIT 38

start something to begin a fight or argument • *He's always starting something – he doesn't know when to keep quiet.* ➔UNIT 6

step up to the plate to take responsibility for doing something • *It is time companies stepped up to the plate and made sure the meat they sell is safe to eat.* ORIGIN: based on the baseball meaning of **step up to the plate** (= move into position to hit the ball) ➔UNIT 30

stick out like a sore thumb to be easily noticed and different • *Ted wore jeans to the party, and he stood out like a sore thumb among all the well-dressed guests.* ➔UNIT 38

stick your neck out, *also* **stick out your neck** to take a risk • *He's shown he's got the courage to stick his neck out to help people.* ➔UNITS 22, 31

stick your nose in something to try to discover things that do not involve you; = **poke your nose into something** ➔UNIT 23

stress you out to make you nervous and tired • *School really stresses me out sometimes.* ➔UNIT 7

strike it rich to become suddenly or unexpectedly rich or successful • *They really struck it rich with that idea.* ➔UNIT 10

strike out to fail • *In the past our ads have been successful, but this time we struck out.* ORIGIN: from an expression used in baseball, referring to a play in which the hitter fails to hit the ball ➔UNIT 25

(as) strong as an ox, *also* **(as) strong as a bull** very strong • *He's one of our best players – strong as an ox, with good speed and great hands.* ORIGIN: based on the idea that an ox is a very strong animal ➔UNIT 32

stuff your face [slang] to eat continuously • *They're home watching the ballgame on TV and stuffing their faces with potato chips.* ➔UNIT 3

stumble across someone/something, *also* **stumble on someone/something** to meet someone or find something unexpectedly • *Lee has stumbled across a plot to sell high-tech U.S. weapons to international terrorists.* ➔UNIT 23

sweep someone off his/her feet to cause someone to fall suddenly and completely in love with you • *You kind of expect to get swept off your feet on Valentine's Day.* ➔UNIT 14

swept away made very emotional or enthusiastic • *You couldn't help feeling swept away by the beauty of the place.* ➔UNIT 4

take a hike, *also* **take a walk** to leave • *He told them, politely but firmly, to take a hike.* • *The manager threatened to take a walk, so the team's owner offered him a better contract.* USAGE: sometimes used as an order: *I don't want to hear excuses Grady – just take a hike.* ➔UNIT 16

take advantage (of someone) to use someone's weakness to improve your own situation • *Mr. Smith often takes advantage of my friendship and leaves the unpleasant tasks for me to do.* ➔UNIT 32

take after someone to be like or look like someone in your family • *Most of our children take after my husband.* ➔UNIT 8

take issue with someone/something to disagree with someone or something • *I take issue with people who say it is unpatriotic to criticize our government.* ➔UNIT 1

take off to suddenly succeed • *The style really took off among teens.* ➔UNIT 33

take on a life of its own to no longer be controlled by anyone • *It was originally Bruce's idea, then it took on a life of its own.* ➔UNIT 30

take on someone, *also* **take someone on** to fight or compete against someone • *Later today, the World Cup champions take on Chile.* ➔UNIT 6

take someone / something for granted to fail to appreciate someone / something • *When your own children are growing up, you tend to take them for granted, and then, suddenly, they are grown up.* ➔UNIT 34

take something with a grain of salt to consider something to be not completely true or right • *I've read the article, which I take with a grain of salt.* ORIGIN: based on the idea that food tastes better and is easier to swallow if you add a little salt ➔UNIT 27

take the bull by the horns to forcefully attack a difficult situation • *I took the bull by the horns and confronted him about his smoking.* ORIGIN: based on the idea that holding a **bull** (= male cow) by its horns is a brave and direct action ➔UNIT 35

take the gloves off to argue or compete without controlling your actions or feelings • *They argued calmly for a while and then they took the gloves off.* ➔UNIT 6

take the plunge to decide to do something • *Those women who took the plunge and ran for the state legislature enjoyed great success.* USAGE: usually said about doing something that involves some risk ➔UNIT 11

take you back (to something) to cause you to remember • *Seeing the movie took me right back to my childhood.* ➔UNIT 29

talk shop to talk about work when not working • *Two New York Yankee pitchers will be there to sign autographs and talk shop with fans.* ➔UNIT 18

tank up on something to drink a great deal of something • *Be sure to tank up on water before you work outdoors on a hot day!* ➔UNIT 3

tear apart someone/something, *also* **tear someone/something apart** to severely criticize someone or something • *His teachers tore him apart for cheating on the test.* ➔UNIT 21

tear yourself away (from someone/something) to force yourself to leave a person, place, or activity • *I'm glad you managed to tear yourself away from the TV and come eat dinner with us.* ➔UNIT 16

tempt fate to take a foolish risk or unnecessary risks • *Don't tempt fate – park under the street light.* ➔UNIT 31

test the waters to try something new • *We are testing the waters to see if online ads increase sales.* ORIGIN: based on the literal meaning of **test the waters** (= to put your toe into water to see how cold it is) ➔UNIT 40

(have) a thick skin be able to ignore personal criticism • *People will tell you they don't like your clothes, your voice, or the color of your eyes, so you need to have a thick skin to survive.* ➔UNIT 12

think outside the box to develop ideas that are different and unusual • *These guys are incredibly creative – they really know how to think outside the box.* ➔UNIT 13

a thorn in the side (of someone/something), *also* **a thorn in someone's/something's side** someone or something that continually causes problems • *Health inspectors are a thorn in the side of most restaurant owners.* ➔UNIT 13

(look) through rose-colored glasses with an attitude that things are better than they really are • *The magazine had a habit of looking at social issues through rose-colored glasses.* ➔UNIT 36

through the wringer experiencing something very difficult or unpleasant • *Mr. Gold went through the wringer to get immigration papers for his parents.* USAGE: usually used with put or go, as in the example ORIGIN: based on the literal meaning of **wringer** (= a device that presses water from clothing that has been washed) ➔UNIT 24

throw a (temper) tantrum to become very angry and unreasonable • *When you are a grown-up, you don't throw a tantrum if something offends you, you discuss it.* ➔UNIT 5

throw a monkey wrench into something to cause something to fail • *We keep trying to get together, but her crazy schedule keeps throwing a monkey wrench into our plans.* ➔UNIT 25

throw cold water on something to criticize or stop something that some people are enthusiastic about • *The proposal seemed reasonable enough, but authorities quickly threw cold water on it.* ➔UNIT 40

throw good money after bad to spend more money on something that has already failed • *If you try to fix that car, you'll simply be throwing good money after bad.* ➔UNIT 10

throw in the towel to admit defeat or failure • *The union was forced to throw in the towel and settle their bitter dispute with the company.* ORIGIN: based on the literal meaning of **throwing a towel into the ring** in boxing (= to signal that a fighter is unable to continue) ➔UNIT 25

throw money at something to try to solve a problem by spending money on it • *You can't create a successful healthcare system by just throwing money at it. It has to be done intelligently.* ➔UNIT 10

throw someone off the scent to give someone false or confusing information so that they will not discover something • *The police were thrown off the scent for a while by two of the witnesses, who were found later to be lying.* ORIGIN: based on the literal meaning of **throw a dog off the scent** (= to cause a dog to lose the smell that leads it to a person or animal) ➔UNIT 23

(give a) thumbs down to someone/something to show disapproval of or opposition to someone or something • *My husband gave a big thumbs down to my idea of getting a new car.* ➔UNIT 38

tip your hand to let others know what you are planning to do • *Some people think he'll announce today that he's quitting, but he certainly didn't tip his hand at yesterday's meeting.* ➔UNIT 11

to die for [slang] extremely good • *We had apple pie, and it was to die for.* ➔UNIT 26

too hot to handle too dangerous or difficult to deal with • *Certain subjects are still too hot to handle on television shows.* ➔UNIT 22

the top of ladder the highest level or position • *After thirty years with the company, he's near the top of the ladder.* ➔UNIT 18

(the) top of the line the very best of something • *The four acts for the opening of the jazz festival were all top of the line.* ➔UNIT 26

touch a (raw) nerve, *also* **hit a (raw) nerve** to cause an emotional reaction • *Any talk of raising the cost of college tuition hits a raw nerve with students.* ➔UNIT 4

touch base (with someone) to talk briefly to someone • *I'll touch base with him later to tell him about the meeting.* ➔UNIT 2

a tough act to follow so good that whatever happens next is not likely to seem as good • *The last mayor was one of the most beloved in the city's history – he was a tough act to follow.* ➔UNIT 26

tough it out to be strong while experiencing difficulties • *Should we tough it out, or should we close the store and go out of business now?* ➔UNIT 32

(as) tough as nails strong and determined • *She is a warm and friendly person, but she is also as tough as nails.* ➔UNIT 32

a tough nut (to crack) a difficult problem to solve • *Unemployment is a tough nut.* ➔UNIT 13

a tough row to hoe a difficult situation to deal with • *The author said that he knew it would be a tough row to hoe when he began research for this book.* ➔UNIT 24

track down someone/something, *also* **track someone/something down** to find someone or something after searching for them • *My mother wanted to find the family who had taken care of my father during the war, and somehow she was able to track them down.* ➔UNIT 23

travel light to take very few things with you when you go on a trip • *My new car has lots of cargo space, which is great for people like me who don't travel light.* ➔UNIT 16

tread water to be active but without making progress or falling farther behind • *Sales are about the same as last year, and the company is only treading water.* ORIGIN: based on the literal meaning of **tread water** (= to stay in one place in water by moving your legs quickly) ➔UNIT 40

try your hand at something to attempt to do something • *Goodwin worked as a journalist, and he also tried his hand at writing fiction for a time.* ➔UNIT 38

turn a profit to earn more money than you spend • *After three years in business, we expected to be turning a profit.* ➔UNIT 10

turn back the clock, *also* **turn the clock back** to make things the same as they were at an earlier time • *Why vote for someone who promises to turn back the clock to better days? That's impossible.* ➔UNIT 15

turn the corner to improve after going through something difficult • *I wonder if the country has really turned the corner in this crisis.* ➔UNIT 24

twist someone's arm to strongly encourage someone to do something they do not want to do • *If he doesn't want to go, you've just got to twist his arm and get him to do it.* ➔UNIT 30

under fire being criticized • *The court is under fire for being too political.* USAGE: often used with **come**: *Johnson has come under fire for gossiping with his clients.* ➔UNIT 21

under someone's/something's thumb, *also* **under the thumb of someone/something** completely controlled by someone or something • *That girl is totally under her mother's thumb.* ➔UNIT 30

under the weather not healthy • *She's not too sick, just a little under the weather.* ➔UNIT 7

until you are blue in the face for a long time • *You can argue until you are blue in the face, but it isn't going to change my opinion.* USAGE: used to suggest that someone will not listen to what is being said ➔UNIT 36

up in arms very angry • *Local businessmen are up in arms over the new parking regulations, which will make shopping very inconvenient for customers.* USAGE: often followed by a phrase beginning with **over** or **about** ➔UNIT 4

up the creek (without a paddle) in an extremely difficult situation • *All those people who have money invested in it are going to be up the creek.* ➔UNIT 13

up to scratch at an acceptable standard or quality • *We're giving him a week to bring the team up to scratch.* USAGE: often used in the form **not up to scratch**: *I'm afraid your essay wasn't up to scratch.* ➔UNIT 26

upset your stomach to make you feel sick • *Something in the sandwich upset my stomach.* ➔UNIT 7

wait on someone hand and foot to do everything for another person • *You should do some of the work around here instead of being waited on hand and foot all the time.* USAGE: often used as a negative remark about someone thought of as unwilling to work ➔UNIT 38

wake up on the wrong side of (the) bed to begin the day feeling unhappy and uncomfortable; = **get up on the wrong side of (the) bed** ➔UNIT 4

walk a tightrope to act carefully to avoid creating enemies or a dangerous situation • *The show has always walked a tightrope between old-fashioned humor and modern comedy.* ORIGIN: from the literal expression **walk a tightrope** (= walk on a tightly stretched wire that is high off the ground) ➔UNIT 22

walk on air to be very happy • *The award winners were walking on air.* ➔UNIT 4

wash down something, *also* **wash something down** to drink a liquid to help you swallow something • *He got two aspirin and washed them down with a glass of water.* ➔UNIT 3

wash out (of something) to leave a program or activity because you failed to meet its standards • *I didn't make it through flight school – I washed out.* ➔UNIT 25

wash your hands of someone/something to end all involvement with someone or something • *Phil seemed cold and distant, and now she was very afraid that he would wash his hands of her.* ➔UNIT 38

watch your step to be careful in a situation that could be dangerous • *You have to watch your step when you're dealing with him, as he has an awful temper.* ➔UNIT 22

water down something, *also* **water something down** to make something weaker • *Some people say the new regulations water down several laws that protect people who rent apartments in the city.* ORIGIN: based on the literal meaning of **water down something** (= to add water to a liquid to weaken things mixed in it) ➔UNIT 40

water under the bridge something that has happened and cannot be changed • *I should probably have asked for more money when I was offered the job, but hey, that's water under the bridge now.* ➔UNIT 40

wave a magic wand to solve a difficult problem with no effort • *Unfortunately, you can't just wave a magic wand and get rid of poverty.* ➔UNIT 13

wear someone out to make someone very tired • *Taking care of two kids all day just wears me out.* ➔UNIT 7

wear the pants (in the family) to be the person in charge in a marriage or family • *She wears the pants in the family.* USAGE: used to describe women ➔UNIT 8

wear your heart on your sleeve to show your feelings, especially love for someone • *You always know where John stands because he wears his heart on his sleeve.* ➔UNIT 5

wet behind the ears young and not experienced • *The job put a lot of responsibility on someone who was still wet behind the ears, but he learned fast.* ➔UNIT 20

whatever floats your boat do what makes you happy • *If you want to take a year off to travel, you should – whatever floats your boat.* ➔UNIT 4

when the chips are down when you are in a difficult or dangerous situation • *When the chips are down, you need people around you that you can depend on.* ➔UNIT 13

when the chips are down when you are in a difficult or dangerous situation • *He's like that special best friend from high school you go to when the chips are down.* ➔UNIT 22

where someone is coming from what causes someone to have a particular opinion • *I can understand where he's coming from, but I don't completely agree with him.* ➔UNIT 1

where there's smoke, there's fire if it looks like something is wrong, something probably is wrong • *People like to think where there's smoke, there's fire, so they will always believe you were involved even if you weren't.* ➔UNIT 37

whip up something, *also* **whip something up** to quickly prepare something to eat • *We were hungry and in a hurry, so Marion whipped up a little snack.* ➔UNIT 3

something will never fly something will not succeed • *People told him it was a great story, but it would never fly as a movie.* ➔UNIT 25

win out to succeed after great effort • *In the end, common sense won out.* →UNIT 33

win someone over, *also* **win over someone** to succeed in changing opinion • *The argument she used to win them over was not about who was right and who was wrong.* →UNIT 1

do something with one hand tied behind your back, *also* **do something with one arm tied behind your back** to do something very easily • *Cleaning your bike is so simple a chimp could do it with one hand tied behind his back.* →UNIT 24

with your back against the wall in a serious situation with few ways to react to it • *The Mexican team has its back against the wall and must win tonight's game.* →UNIT 13

do something with your eyes closed to do something very easily • *I've filled this form in so many times, I could do it with my eyes closed.* →UNIT 24

work hand in glove with someone/something to do something together with someone or something else • *The computer chips are designed to work hand in glove with the new microprocessor.* USAGE: often used in the form **go hand in glove** →UNIT 18

the world is your oyster you have the ability and the freedom to do exactly what you want • *The world is your oyster when you're young and healthy and free to go anywhere.* →UNIT 19

worth a damn [slang] to have value • *Kids in this city aren't getting an education that's worth a damn.* →UNIT 34

(it's well) worth it it is rewarding despite the difficulties involved • *It was a long climb up the hill, but the view from the top was worth it.* →UNIT 34

worth its weight in gold extremely useful or valuable • *User-friendly software is worth its weight in gold.* ORIGIN: based on the idea that gold is the most valuable metal →UNIT 26

you bet I agree • *"I think people in that neighborhood are snobs." "Oh, you bet."* →UNIT 1

you can say that again, *also* **you said it** [especially spoken] I agree with you completely • *"That was an absolutely delicious lunch." "You can say that again."* →UNIT 1

Answer key

Unit 1 Agreeing and disagreeing

Focus on meaning

A. Grouping

Agreeing: a, d, g, k, l

Disagreeing: b, c, j, m

Opinions: e, f, h, i

B. Matching

1.b 2. c 3. g 4. e 5. d 6. a 7. f

Focus on form

A. Scrambled sentences

1. That is one issue we see eye to eye on.
2. You have got to be kidding!
3. On the contrary, we think it's a very good idea.
4. Can I just put my two cents in?
5. You can say that again.
6. If you don't agree, speak up.

B. Sentence completion

1. same 2. issue 3. over 4. where 5. take 6. out 7. with 8. piece 9. You 10. And

Focus on use

A. Formality

1. a 2. b 3. a

Unit 2 Communicating

Focus on meaning

A. Grouping

Talking or telling: b, e, f
Listening to or trying to get someone to talk: d
Not talking: a
Receiving information: c

B. Matching

1. e 2. f 3. a 4. d 5. c 6. h 7. b 8. g

Focus on form

A. Communicating crossword

Across: 3. compare 4. between 6. let 7. pick

Down: 1. draw 2. open 4. bite 5. touch 6. loop 8. in

B. Correct or incorrect?

1. ✘ – Stay in touch! 2. ✘ – Stop beating around the bush. 3. ✔ 4. ✔ 5. ✘ – He really opened up and talked about everything. 6. ✔ 7. ✔ 8. ✘ – She's always ready to lend an ear when it's needed.

Focus on use

A. Formality

1. clammed up 2. beat around the bush 3. compare notes 4. gotten wind of

Unit 3 Eating and drinking

Focus on meaning

A. Matching

1. b 2. c 3. h 4. f 5. a 6. i 7. e 8. j 9. g 10. d

B. Sentence completion

1. whipped up 2. ate us out of house and home 3. ate like a horse 4. picked at 5. pigged out

Focus on form

A. Prepositions and adverbs

1. with 2. to 3. away 4. down with 5. up on 6. at 7. out

B. Scrambled sentences

1. She eats like a horse but she stays thin. *or* She stays thin but she eats like a horse.
2. Drowning your sorrows is not a good idea.
3. Let's go home and I'll whip something up. *or* Let's go home and I'll whip up something.
4. They stayed with us for two weeks and ate us out of house and home.
5. We went to the movies and stuffed our faces with popcorn.
6. She likes to pig out on junk food sometimes. *or* She sometimes likes to pig out on junk food.

Focus on use

A. Formality

1. a, c, m 2. all 3. a, b, c 4. a, b, c, m

Unit 4 Feelings

Focus on meaning

A. Positive or negative?

1. P 2. N 3. N 4. N 5. P 6. N 7. P 8. N

B. Sentence completion

1. Whatever floats your boat 2. on edge 3. cool off 4. blowing hot and cold 5. a lump in my throat 6. carried away 7. up in arms 8. choked up 9. picks you up 10. touched a raw nerve

Focus on form

A. Prepositions and adverbs

1. down 2. up 3. in 4. in 5. over 6. of 7. away 8. up, on, of 9. on 10. up

B. Correct or incorrect?

1. ✘ – Are you on edge before an exam?
2. ✘ – We are up in arms about the plan.
3. ✔ 4. ✔ 5. ✘ – He's down in the dumps.
6. ✘ – He blows hot and cold all the time.
7. ✘ – Winning really picked us up.
8. ✘ – You're a sight for sore eyes! 9. ✔

Focus on use

A. Formality

1. down in the dumps 2. on edge 3. driving me up the wall 4. up in arms 5. a sight for sore eyes 6. picked me up

Unit 5 Expressing emotions

Focus on meaning

A. Matching

1. g 2. i 3. e 4. b 5. a 6. h 7. j 8. d 9. c 10. f.

B. Grouping

Expressing happiness: be all smiles, dissolve into laughter, light up

Controlling emotions: get a grip (on yourself), keep a straight face

Expressing sadness / anger: dissolve into tears, go ballistic, lose your head

Focus on form

A. Feelings crossword

Across: 3. sleeve 4. straight 8. grip 9. steam

Down: 1. dissolved 2. chest 4. smiles 5. guard 6. temper 7. bare

B. Correct or incorrect?

1. ✔ 2. ✘ – There were gales of laughter coming from the classroom. 3. ✔ 4. ✘ – Suddenly their faces just lit up. 5. ✔ 6. ✘ – They burst (*or* dissolved) into tears when they heard the news. 7. ✔ 8. ✔

Focus on use

A. Sentence completion

Possible answers: 1. lost (my) temper *or* lost (my) head 2. go ballistic 3. get (things) off my chest 4. let off (some) steam *or* blow off some steam

Unit 6 Fighting and arguing

Focus on meaning

A. Which idiom?

1. c 2. c 3. c 4. a 5. c 6. b 7. a 8. a

B. Matching

1. e 2. a 3. b 4. f 5. d 6. g 7. c
Missing word: fight

Focus on form

A. Prepositions

1. on 2. for 3. out 4. on 5. to 6. off 7. at 8. with

B. Scrambled sentences

1. They've had a running battle for years.

2. The argument is hot and heavy.

3. She really let him have it!

4. The referees tried to keep the peace.

5. Do you want to start something?

6. Don't pick a fight with him!

Focus on use

A. Time line

1. spoiling for a fight 2–3. pick a fight, start something 4. take someone on 5–6. come to blows, let someone have it 7. going at it 8–10. fight it out, hot and heavy, take the gloves off

Unit 7 Health

Focus on meaning

A. Connections

1. feel well 2. make you feel good 3. feel weak or ill 4. seriously ill 5. cause you to feel ill 6. resist an illness 7. become ill 8. signs that you are not well 9. become healthier

B. Scrambled dialog

1. e 2. c 3. d 4. a 5. b

Focus on form

A. Sentence completion

1. down, flu 2. under, weather 3. bill, health
4. fighting, lives 5. bags, eyes 6. back, feet
7. stress, out 8. upsets, stomach

B. Correct or incorrect?

1. ✘ – on 2. ✔ 3. ✘ – up 4. ✔ 5. ✘ – the
6. ✔ 7. ✘ – on 8. ✔

Focus on use

A. Formality

1. under the weather 2. fighting off
3. stressing me out 4. wearing me out
5. did me a world of good 6. got over
7. back on my feet

Unit 8 Home and family

Focus on meaning

Concept map

1. p 2–4. a, k, n 5. d 6. e 7. o 8. f 9. b
10–11. c, g 12–13. l, m 14. i 15. h 16. j

Focus on form

A. Editing

1. settle down

2. takes after

3. our nearest and dearest

4. at home

5. thicker than water

6. born with a silver spoon in her mouth

7. settling in

8. handed down

B. Sentence completion

1. chip, block 2. pull, roots
3. home, home 4. put, roots
5. run, family 6. flown, nest
7. wears, pants 8. bosom, family

Focus on use

A. Letter from home

1. settling in 2. at home 3. settle down
4. left *or* flown the nest 5. runs in the family *or* runs in your dad's family

Unit 9 Learning and studying

Focus on meaning

Paraphrasing

Your answers may be different, but here are some possible responses:

1. When we first met them, they seemed like the perfect neighbors.
2. Make sure you study about local history before the quiz.
3. Most of us need to do more work on our computer skills.
4. We learned our multiplication tables by memorizing them.
5. It was clear that she had read about the subject before the meeting.
6. The safety procedures were repeated to us again and again.
7. You can't trust the department head. I know that because of a bad experience I had.
8. I'm not going to spend more than I can afford. I've done it before, and it wasn't a good idea.
9. He's been working here for only two weeks. He's still learning how we do things.
10. We're having trouble learning English, but our kids have learned it quickly from their friends.
11. It's worth learning about the museums in the city.
12. My sister likes studying in classrooms, but I prefer to sit in sidewalk cafés and learn the language by hearing and speaking it.

Focus on form

A. Learning and studying crossword

Across: 1. blush 3. lesson 5. rote
6. read 7. soak

Down: 1. brush 2. homework 4. ropes

B. Sentence completion

1. drilled into 2. Learning the ropes 3. picked (it) up 4. found out the hard way 5. bone up on 6. learned my lesson

Unit 10 Money

Focus on meaning

A. Sentence completion

1. turn a profit 2. get your money's worth
3. throwing good money after bad 4. money is no object 5. break even 6. bring home the bacon

B. Odd one out

1. c 2. c 3. b 4. c 5. a

Focus on form

A. Correct or incorrect?

1. ✔ 2. ✘ – When things started to go wrong, he just threw money at it. 3. ✘ – She's pulling down about $80,000 a year. 4. ✔ 5. ✘ – Their company was the first one to turn a profit. 6. ✔

B. Prepositions and adverbs

1. up 2. down 3. at 4. after 5. in 6. to

Focus on use

A. Formality

1. breaking even 2. turning a profit
3. making a killing, striking it rich, *or* cleaning up 4. get their money's worth 5. an arm and a leg

Unit 11 Negotiations and decisions

Focus on meaning

Concept map

1. c 2–3. i, m 4. n 5–7. e, g, k 8. h 9. b 10. d 11. f 12. a 13. l 14. j

Focus on form

A. Scrambled story

1, 6, 5, 2, 4, 3, 7

B. Correct or incorrect?

1. ✘ – We're between a rock and a hard place. 2. ✔ 3. ✘ – Let's split the difference and set the price at $150. 4. ✔ 5. ✘ – OK, you can go, but it's against our / my better judgment. 6. ✔ 7. Stop beating around the bush.

Unit 12 Personality and character

Focus on meaning

A. Sentence completion

1. a heart of stone 2. blessed with 3. have a dishonest bone in his body 4. at peace with herself 5. comes across as 6. at my best 7. have a thick skin 8. in my blood

B. Correct or incorrect?

Possible answers: 1. ✘ – Helen and Brian are good and ordinary people. 2. ✔ 3. ✘ – He did not speak much. 4. ✘ – He acts angry *or* He is easily upset. 5. ✔ 6. ✘ – I don't like him because he thinks he's so important.

Focus on form

A. Sentence transformation

1. Margot is blessed with unlimited energy and enthusiasm.
2. Murat comes across as lazy.
3. Karla is as honest as they come. *or* Karla is as trustworthy as they come.
4. He doesn't have many friends because he's so full of himself.
5. He was more at peace with himself as he got older.

B. Sentence completion

Possible answers:

1. David is successful in business because he has a heart of stone.
2. Katya doesn't have an unkind bone in her body.
3. Go to bed early so you will be at your best for the interview tomorrow.
4. Barry has a chip on his shoulder.
5. Farmers are the salt of the earth.
6. Penny has a thick skin.

Focus on use

A. Dialog completion

Possible answers:

1. He doesn't have a conceited bone in his body.
2. No, he comes across that way, but he's actually very nice.
3. He's as generous as they come.

Unit 13 Problems and solutions

Focus on meaning

A. Correct or incorrect?

1. ✘ – The team has a problem. 2. ✔ 3. ✘ – I wish I could solve this problem (with no effort). 4. ✔ 5. ✔ 6. ✘ – Kate has been a continuing problem.

B. Odd one out

1. b 2. c 3. c 4. b 5. c 6. a

Focus on form

A. Prepositions and adverbs

1. over 2. down 3. up with 4. up 5. in 6. outside 7. against 8. in

B. Key words

1. put our heads together 2. (have) saved the day 3. papering over 4. thinking outside the box 5. wave a magic wand 6. in dire straits

Focus on use

A. Formality

1. a tough nut to crack 2. in dire straits 3. your back is against the wall 4. save the day 5. paper over 6. come up with

Unit 14 Relationships

Focus on meaning

Super crossword

Across: 4. build 5. sweep 7. rocks 9. hit 10. mend 11. fall 12. hung

Down: 1. bad 2. lose 3. keep 4. back 6. part 8. common 9. heels 11. first

Focus on form

A. What's wrong with these sentences?

1. We just didn't hit it off. 2. We need to mend fences (*or* build bridges) between divisions. 3. Try to keep him at arm's length. 4. We go back a long way. 5. It's obvious that their marriage is on the rocks. 6. Is it too late to mend fences with your ex-husband? 7. We knew it was time to part company. 8. Let's fall in love! 9. I lost my heart.

B. Pronunciation love song

1. head over heels 2. swept off your feet 3. love at first sight 4. hung up on 5. in common 6. got it bad

Unit 15 Time

Focus on meaning

A. Time line

The past affecting the present: turn back the clock, make up for lost time

The present (now): at the moment, the here and now, for the time being

The future: down the line, drop-dead date, in the fullness of time

B. Time scale

Always: day and night, around the clock

Sometimes: (every) now and then

Rarely: once in a blue moon

C. Correct or incorrect?

1. ✘ – He cannot take care of himself. 2. ✔ 3. ✔ 4. ✘ – They expect big sales later. 5. ✔ 6. ✔

Focus on form

A. Prepositions and adverbs

1. up, for 2. in 3. around 4. at 5. in 6. in 7. back

B. Sentence transformation

1. The rescue team has been working day and night.
2. The drop-dead date for this assignment is June 2.
3. He has been dishonest all along.
4. We're happy living here for the time being.
5. Remember to e-mail us every now and then!
6. They advised us to forget about the past and to concentrate on the here and now.
7. I'd quit this job and take that one in a heartbeat if they offered it to me.

Focus on use

A. Formality

Possible answers:

1. around the clock *or* day and night
2. around the clock
3. at the moment *or* for the time being
4. for the long haul

5. in the long run *or* in the long term *or* down the line *or* in the fullness of time

6. once in a blue moon

7. in a (New York) minute *or* in a heartbeat

Unit 16 Travel

Focus on meaning

A. Odd one out

1. b 2. c 3. a 4. c 5. c

B. Sentence completion

1. get itchy feet 2. off the beaten track, get away from it all 3. tear yourself away, hit the road 4. travel light 5. set off

Focus on form

A. Traveling and going places crossword

Across: 3. off 4. beaten 7. duck 8. itchy 10. over 11. tear

Down: 1. light 2. hike 3. on 5. away 6. set 7. door 9. hit

B. Scrambled story

1, 6, 3, 2, 5, 4, 7

Focus on use

A. Formality

1. slipped out 2. tear himself away 3. showed him the door 4. take a hike

Unit 17 Understanding

Focus on meaning

A. Grouping

Understand: b, c, d, e, f, g, n

Not understand: a, h, i, j, k, l, m, o, p

B. Odd one out

1. a 2. c 3. c 4. c 5. c

Focus on form

A. Prepositions

1. on 2. beyond 3. out 4. with 5. on 6. around 7. over

B. Missing verbs

1. connect 2. were 3. get *or* catch 4. get 5. go 6. losing 7. missing 8. put

Focus on use

A. Formality

1. get a fix on 2. was none the wiser 3. beyond me 4. connected the dots 5. put two and two together

Unit 18 Work

Focus on meaning

Matching

1. o 2. a 3. f 4. g 5. h 6. e 7. j 8. d 9. i 10. l 11. p 12. k 13. n 14. c 15. b 16. m

Focus on form

A. Sentence completion

1. work, play 2. roll, sleeves 3. work, out 4. fill, for 5. over, head 6. hand, glove 7. all, day's 8. bottom, ladder

B. Correct or incorrect?

1. ✔ 2. ✘ – in 3. ✘ – on 4. ✔ 5. ✔ 6. ✘ – about 7. ✔

Focus on use

A. Formality

1. filling in 2. all in a day's work 3. go over Jane's head 4. been falling down on the job 5. rolling her sleeves up *or* rolling up her sleeves

Unit 19 Ability

Focus on meaning

Matching

1. e 2. k 3. l 4. f 5. b 6. c 7. d 8. i 9. a 10. n 11. j 12. h 13. g 14. m

Focus on form

A. Sentence completion

1. got, feel 2. mind, own 3. has, nose 4. feeling, oats 5. seat, pants 6. born, to 7. run, rings 8. world, oyster

B. Prepositions

1. on 2. for 3. with 4. through 5. in 6. in

Focus on use

A. Formality

1. put you through your paces 2. flying by the seat of our pants 3. had it in us 4. ran rings around 5. has a head for *or* was born to 6. have a nose for finding

Unit 20 Age

Focus on meaning

A. Matching

1. b 2. a 3. c 4. e 5. d 6. h 7. f 8. g

B. Sentence completion

1. seen better days 2. wet behind the ears 3. live in the past 4. of a certain age, put out to pasture 5. behind the times 6. old as the hills 7. on its last legs 8. getting on (in) years

Focus on form

A. Prepositions

1. behind 2. out to 3. from 4. past 5. on 6. in 7. in 8. behind

B. Correct or incorrect

1. ✘ – out 2. ✔ 3. ✔ 4. ✘ – out 5. ✘ – is 6. ✘ – to 7. ✘ – from

Focus on use

A. Formality

1. on its last legs 2. seen better days 3. past my prime 4. getting on in years 5. put you out to pasture 6. a blast from the past

Unit 21 Criticism

Focus on meaning

Concept map

1. c 2. e 3. g 4. h 5. b 6. j 7. o 8. l 9. k 10. m 11. d 12. a 13. n 14. f 15. i

Focus on form

A. Beginnings and endings

1. i 2. h 3. b 4. c 5. f 6. e 7. d 8. g 9. a

B. Preposition crossword

Across: 1. under 3. on 4. after

Down: 1. up 2. down 3. over

Focus on use

A. What do you say?

Suggested answers: 1. biting the hand that feeds you 2. look a gift horse in the mouth 3. make fun of him 4. draw (some) fire *or* come under fire 5. in the line of fire 6. tear it apart

Unit 22 Danger

Focus on meaning

A. Grouping

1. g, h, i, j 2. a, e, k 3. c, d, n 4. b, f, l, m

B. Sentence completion

1. on the loose 2. blow the whistle 3. put (their) lives on the line 4. on her guard

Focus on form

A. Danger crossword

Across: 1. walk 4. play 5. jeopardy 7. whistle 10. neck

Down: 2. line 3. handle 6. open 7. watch 8. stick 9. loose

B. Scrambled sentences

1. Quick – hit the deck!
2. You need to be on your guard all the time.
3. The kid threw a snowball, so I hit the dirt.
4. She's a great friend when the chips are down.

Focus on use

A. Describing danger

Possible answers: 1. walking a tightrope 2. stick his neck out *or* risk his neck 3. on their guard 4. in jeopardy 5. watch their step 6. on the loose 7. when the chips are down.

Unit 23 Search and Discover

Focus on meaning

Correct or incorrect?

1. ✘ – It's extremely difficult to find anything in his office. 2. ✘ – They found him in a hotel downtown after searching for him. 3. ✘ – She unexpectedly found an old letter of his. 4. ✘ – Their job is to find talented new singers. 5. ✘ – The police were misled by two of the witnesses. 6. ✔ 7. ✔ 8. ✔ 9. ✔ 10. ✔ 11. ✔

Focus on form

A. Prepositions and adverbs

1. down 2. on 3. out 4. between 5. out 6. to 7. in 8. into

B. Beginnings and endings

1. f 2. c 3. d 4. a 5. b 6. e

Focus on use

A. Sentence completion

Suggested answers: 1. stumbled across 2. track down 3. needle in a haystack 4. beating the bushes

Unit 24 Easy / difficult

Focus on meaning

Concept map

1. f, g 2. e, i 3. a, b, k 4. m 5. o 6. d 7. n 8. h, j 9. l 10. c

Focus on form

Sentence completion

1. easy 2. cake 3. row 4. mud 5. plain 6. eyes 7. behind 8. wheels 9. rocket 10. pulling 11. candy 12. roses 13. path 14. through 15. corner

Focus on use

A. Sentence completion

Possible answers: 1. taking candy from a baby 2. pulling teeth 3. tough row to hoe 4. easy as pie 5. piece of cake 6–7. with one hand / arm tied behind your back *or* with your eyes closed 8. clear as mud 9. plain as day 10. through the wringer

Unit 25 Failure

Focus on meaning

Sentence transformation

Possible answers:

1. It was my first public presentation, and I was worried that I would fall flat on my face.
2. It's just not good enough – we'll have to go back to the drawing board.

3. She watched her parents' marriage crash and burn.
4. We try to psych the other team out *or* psych out the other team before the game begins.
5. People told him it was a great story but it wouldn't (*or* would never) fly as a movie.
6. In the past, our ads have been successful, but this time we struck out.
7. The union had to throw in the towel and settle its dispute with the company.
8. Public schools have dropped the ball on arts education.
9. We keep trying to get together, but her crazy schedule keeps throwing a monkey wrench into our plans.
10. His business is going down the tubes, and he's about to lose his house.
11. His career really hit the skids after his divorce.
12. All their plans suddenly blew up in their faces.

Focus on form

A. Beginnings and endings

1. d 2. f 3. a 4. h 5. i 6. c 7. k 8. m 9. o 10. g 11. n 12. e *or* j 13. b 14. l 15. e *or* j

B. Correct or incorrect?

1. ✘ – to 2. ✔ 3. ✔ 4. ✘ – over 5. ✘ – on

Focus on use

A. What do you say?

Possible answers:

1. Well, it's back to the drawing board, then.
2. Try not to drop the ball.
3. Don't let her psych you out.
4. We all strike out sometimes.
5. Yes, the school is coming apart at the seams.

Unit 26 Good and Bad

Focus on meaning

A. Matching

1. the bottom of the barrel – 2. worth its weight in gold + 3. make your mouth water + 4. a tough act to follow + 5. the greatest thing since sliced bread + 6. the bottom of the heap –

B. Correct or incorrect?

1. ✘ – He's better than the others. 2. ✘ – Business was bad before, and it has gotten worse. 3. ✔ 4. ✔ 5. ✘ – The chocolate cake is delicious.

Focus on form

A. Prepositions

1. of 2. above 3. of 4. of 5. to 6. up, to 7. from, to 8. up 9. about

B. Beginnings and endings

1. g 2. d 3. a 4. e 5. f 6. c 7. b.

Focus on use

Describing good and bad

Possible idioms used include: 1. tough act to follow 2. to die for *or* makes your mouth water 3. went from bad to worse 4. not all it's cracked up to be *or* nothing to write home about 5. worth its weight in gold 6. cream of the crop *or* the top of the line *or* heads and shoulders above the rest

Unit 27 Honesty

Focus on meaning

Concept map

1. a 2. b 3. n 4. e 5. o 6. f 7. g 8. j 9. k 10. c 11. i 12. h 13. m 14. l 15. d

Focus on form

A. Detective story

1. true 2. salt 3. level 4. bottom 5. pull 6. call 7. line 8. clean 9. record 10. on 11. bones 12. bottom

B. Scrambled sentences

1. There is something about his story that rings hollow.
2. They beat us fair and square.
3. The news reporter didn't pull any punches.
4. Everything about the business is on the level. *or* Everything is on the level about the business.
5. I intend to get to the bottom of this.

Focus on use

A. Formality

Suggested answers:

1. My references are from two of my professors, and I think what they say about me is true.
2. I should mention that I have applied to the Good Student Scholarship Fund once before.
3. I would be grateful for the opportunity the scholarship would give me.
4. Thank you very much.

Unit 28 Knowledge

Focus on meaning

A. Odd one out

1. b 2. c 3. c 4. b 5. c

B. Sentence completion

1. like the back of his (*or* her) hand 2. out of my depth 3. had it down pat 4. finger on the pulse 5. the faintest idea

Focus on form

A. Correct or incorrect?

1. ✘ – Don't worry, I know this neighborhood like the back of my hand. 2. ✔ 3. ✘ – When the discussion turned to politics, I was out of my depth. 4. ✔ 5. ✘ – I could feel it in my bones. 6. ✘ – They have their finger on the pulse of teenage fashion. 7. ✘ – People in the know say that he is guilty. 8. ✘ – He used to go to the gym for free until the staff got wise to him.

B. Knowledge crossword

Across: 3. beats 6. inside 8. guess 9. track

Down: 1. clue 2. down 4. abreast 5. stuff 7. idea

Focus on use

A. Formality

1. be an expert 2. knows nothing about 3. I do not understand 4. know about 5. No one knows

Unit 29 Memory

Focus on meaning

A. Matching

1. e 2. a 3. g 4. f 5. d 6. b 7. c

B. Grouping

1. remember something 2. cause someone to remember something 3. forget 4. memorize 5. try to remember

Focus on form

A. Prepositions and adverbs

1. in 2. back 3. of 4. to 5. on 6. to 7. at *or* in 8. back

B. Beginnings and endings

1. c 2. g 3. a 4. h 5. f 6. b 7. e 8. d

Focus on use

A. Politeness

1. b (a is rude) 2. a (b is rude) 3. a (b is a bit rude) 4. b (a is rude)

Unit 30 Responsibility and control

Focus on meaning

A. Matching

1. f 2. g 3. h 4. i 5. b 6. c 7. d 8. a 9. e

B. Sentence transformation

1. Now that you're in management, you've got to start calling the shots.
2. Our new teacher walked in the first day and laid down the law.
3. Just leave them to their own devices.
4. Once an earthquake starts, it takes on a life of its own.
5. The kids always get their own way.

Focus on form

A. Beginnings and endings

1. f 2. g 3. b 4. a 5. h 6. d 7. c 8. e

B. Prepositions

1. off 2. under 3. at 4. up, to 5. in 6. on, of 7. down

Focus on use

A. Formality

Possible answers: 1. take over his (*or* her) responsibilities 2. allowed us to make our own decisions 3. took responsibility 4. making (management) decisions 5. take responsibility for getting things done

Unit 31 Risks and opportunities

Focus on meaning

Concept map

1–3. a, c, j 4. i 5. l 6. k 7. m 8. f 9. b 10. g 11. h 12. d 13. n 14. e

Focus on form

A. Prepositions

1. in 2. for 3. at 4. in 5. out 6. on 7. through 8. out

B. Scrambled sentences

1. Dad thinks I should play it safe.
2. Don't bet the ranch!
3. I think you're tempting fate.
4. Reply today so that you don't miss the boat.
5. We'll win, given half a chance.
6. Would you stick your neck out for this deal?
7. You're out of luck this time.
8. I'd jump at the chance!

Focus on use

A. Risk questionnaire

Give yourself 1 point for each *a*, 3 points for each *b*, and 5 points for each *c*. Add up your points to get your total score.

14–20 You are a major risk taker. You do not like to miss the boat, ever!

8–13 You are a moderate risk-taker. You like to reduce risks, but you're willing to take a chance now and then.

4–7 You don't like taking risks. You like to play it really, really safe.

Unit 32 Strength and weakness

Focus on meaning

A. Physical or mental?

Physical: b, d **Mental/emotional:** a, c, e, f

B. Correct or incorrect?

1. ✔ 2. ✔ 3. ✘ – The agreement is weak.
4. ✘ – I didn't want to seem too forceful.
5. ✘ – They use part-time teachers. 6. ✔
7. ✘ – I suggest you try to be strong. 8. ✘ –
Their team was strong and determined.

Focus on form

A. Odd one out – pronunciation

1. a 2. b 3. a 4. b 5. a 6. a

B. Beginnings and endings

1. h 2. e 3. b 4. f 5. g 6. d 7. c 8. a

Focus on use

A. What do you say?

Possible answers:

1. Thank you. You've been a pillar of strength.
2. You need to make your presence felt.
3. Thanks – your review was a real shot in the arm.
4. It's mind over matter. We're going to tough it out.

Unit 33 Success

Focus on meaning

A. Matching

1. f 2. d 3. a 4. e 5. c 6. b

B. Odd one out

1. b 2. b 3. c 4. b

Focus on form

A. Prepositions and adverbs

1. off 2. out 3. off 4. through 5. off 6. off 7. by

B. Beginnings and endings

1. c 2. f 3. b 4. h 5. a 6. e 7. d 8. g

Focus on use

A. What do you say?

Possible answers:

1. Great! You've had the last laugh.
2. I sailed through it.
3. Congratulations – you won out in the end.
4. You'd better work hard – you just scraped by last year.
5. That's a great idea – I'm sure you'll make a go of it.
6. We really hit pay dirt.

Unit 34 Value

Focus on meaning

Sentence transformation

Possible answers:

1. This is a great little camera that gives you a lot of bang for your / the buck.
2. I wonder if I got my money's worth.
3. When the bottom fell out of the real estate market, a lot of people lost a lot of money.
4. She decided to sell her stocks because she felt the market was going south.
5. Stocks picked up speed in the final hour of trading this afternoon.
6. So many of us take clean water for granted.
7. The landlord's promises are not worth the paper they are printed on.
8. The case made a mockery of the legal process.

9. Some people look down on the homeless.
10. The beauty of the Internet is its openness.
11. Kids in this city aren't getting an education that's worth a damn.
12. It was a long climb up the hill, but the view from the top was (well) worth it.
13. When you're a kid, you take your parents for granted.

Focus on form

A. Correct or incorrect?

1. ✘ – down 2. ✔ 3. ✘ – to 4. ✘ – the 5. ✘ – far

B. Spell check

1. b 2. a 3. c 4. a 5. c 6. c 7. a 8. c

Focus on use

A. Virus alert!

Suggested answers:

1. bang for your buck 2. picking up speed 3. bottom fell out of 4. not worth the paper they are printed on

B. Over to you

Possible answers:

a. Something may appear to be valuable but is not really valuable.

b. Something that you definitely have is worth more than something you might get.

c. Don't assume, before a project is finished, that it will be a success.

d. Don't risk everything in support of one idea or plan.

Unit 35 Animals

Focus on meaning

Sentence completion

1. straight from the horse's mouth 2. for the birds 3. let the cat out of the bag 4. beating a dead horse 5. got off his high horse 6. his bark is worse than his bite 7. other fish to fry 8. took the bull by the horns 9. gone to the dogs 10. call off the dogs 11. horsing around 12. putting the cart before the horse 13. bird's-eye-view 14. in the doghouse 15. fish or cut bait

Focus on form

A. Beginnings and endings

1. b 2. e 3. i 4. h 5. c 6. j 7. d 8. g 9. a 10. f

B. Pronunciation

1. beating a dead horse 2. the cat is out of the bag 3. got other fish to fry 4. for the birds 5. straight from the horse's mouth

Focus on use

A. What's your advice?

Suggested answers:

1. c 2. a 3. b

Unit 36 Colors

Focus on meaning

A. In other words

1. a 2. a 3. b 4. a 5. b 6. b 7. a

B. Sentence completion

1. blacked out 2. paint the town red 3. in the black 4. green with envy 5. the pot calling the kettle black 6. a bolt from the blue 7. in the pink 8. out of the blue

Focus on form

A. Which color – black, blue, green, or red?

1. black 2. blue 3. black 4. blue 5. red 6. red 7. red 8. green

B. Colors crossword

Across: 4. glasses 6. the

Down: 1. white 2. light 3. black 5. see

Focus on use

A. What do you say?

Possible answers:

1. He's been looking at it through rose-colored glasses.
2. Let's go out and paint the town red.
3. Absolutely. It was like a bolt from the blue. *or* It came out of the blue.
4. You really should wait until you have something in black and white.

Unit 37 Fire and smoke

Focus on meaning:

Matching

1. o 2. j 3. m 4. n 5. i 6. k 7. h 8. g 9. p 10. c 11. b 12. f 13. a 14. e 15. l 16. d

Focus on form

A. Prepositions

1. out, into 2. with 3. up, in 4. in 5. on 6. with 7. under 8. out

B. Sentence completion

1. added 2. held *or* put 3. burned 4. fanning 5. smoke 6. smoke, fire 7. blowing 8. went

Focus on use

A. Formality

1. going out of the frying pan into the fire
2. go up in smoke 3. light a fire under him (*also possible*: hold his feet to the fire)
4. blowing smoke 5. hold his feet to the fire (*also possible*: light a fire under him)
6. several irons in the fire

Unit 38 Hands and shoulders

Focus on meaning

A. Beginnings and endings

1. b 2. d 3. e 4. a 5. c 6. g 7. h 8. f 9. k 10. l 11. j 12. i 13. o 14. m 15. n

B. Sentence completion

1. give me a hand 2. thumbs up 3. had a hand in 4. had / got my hands full

Focus on form

A. Hands and shoulders crossword

Across: 2. sore 3. wait 5. lend 6. keep 7. wash

Down: 1. shoulder 2. stand 4. thumbs 8. at

B. Correct or incorrect?

1. ✔ 2. ✘ – of 3. ✔ 4. ✔ 5. ✘ – a 6. ✔ 7. ✘ – the

Focus on use

A. What do you say?

Possible answers:

1. Let me give you a hand.
2. You need a shoulder to cry on.
3. Why not try your hand at something simple?
4. We'll stand shoulder to shoulder with you.
5. You should stop waiting on him hand and foot.
6. You should wash your hands of him.

Unit 39 Feet and legs

Focus on meaning

Which definition?

1. a 2. b 3. a 4. a 5. a 6. a 7. b 8. b
9. b 10. a 11. b 12. b 13. a 14. b 15. a

Focus on form

A. Prepositions

1. on 2. forward 3 down, on 4. up 5. on
6. on 7. off, on 8. in

B. Sentence completion

1. dragging, heels 2. find, feet 3. got, right
4. get, wet 5. jumped, both 6. pulling, leg

Focus on use

A. What's your advice?

Possible answers:

1. Take some time to find your feet, then go ahead and join a club.
2. It's time for him to stand on his own two feet. *or* Put your foot down and tell him he can either pay the rent or move out.
3. Be careful! It's important to put your best foot forward. *or* No, you will probably get off on the wrong foot.

Unit 40 Water and waves

Focus on meaning

Key words

1. d, j 2. a 3. c, h 4. g 5. l 6. b, e 7. k 8. f
9. o 10. m 11. i 12. n

Focus on form

A. Water or wave?

1. water 2. water 3. water 4. wave 5. water
6. water 7. waves 8. waters 9. water
10. wave 11. waters 12. water

B. Prepositions

1. on 2. down 3. under 4. out, of 5. in
6. in 7. of 8. between

Focus on use

A. What do you say?

Possible answers:
1. It doesn't hold water. 2. You're going to end up in hot water. 3. It's water under the bridge. 4. Test the waters. 5. Don't muddy the waters. 6. Don't make waves.

Notes

It's a good idea to keep a record of new idioms as you learn them.
Use this grid to make remembering and reviewing idioms quick, easy, and effective.

Topic (for example: 'feeling')	Idiom	Meaning	Used in a sentence	Translation (if you're sure!)

Track Listing for Audio CD

Track	Unit	Page
1	1 - Agreeing and disagreeing	2
2	2 - Communicating	6
3	3 - Eating and drinking	10
4	4 - Feelings	14
5	5 - Expressing emotions	18
6	6 - Fighting and arguing	22
7	7 - Health	26
8	8 - Home and family	30
9	9 - Learning and studying	34
10	10 - Money	38
11	11 - Negotiations and decisions	42
12	12 - Personality and character	46
13	13 - Problems and solutions	50
14	14 - Relationships	54
15	15 - Time	58
16	16 - Travel	62
17	17 - Understanding	66
18	18 - Work	70
19	19 - Ability	74
20	20 - Age	78
21	21 - Criticism	82
22	22 - Danger	86
23	23 - Search and discover	90
24	24 - Easy / difficult	94
25	25 - Failure	98
26	26 - Good and bad	102
27	27 - Honesty	106
28	28 - Knowledge	110
29	29 - Memory	114
30	30 - Responsibility and control	118
31	31 - Risks and opportunities	122
32	32 - Strength and weakness	126
33	33 - Success	130
34	34 - Value	134
35	35 - Animals	138
36	36 - Colors	142
37	37 - Fire and smoke	146
38	38 - Hands and shoulders	150
39	39 - Feet and legs	154
40	40 - Water and waves	158